A
PILGRIM
PRIESTHOOD

Rangd Patterson

1 Peter 3:15

A
PILGRIM
PRIESTHOOD

*An Exposition
of the Epistle of First Peter*

Paige Patterson

THOMAS NELSON PUBLISHERS
Nashville • Camden • New York

Published in Nashville, Tennessee, by Thomas Nelson, Inc. and distributed in Canada by Lawson Falle, Ltd., Cambridge, Ontario.

Printed in the United States of America.

Unless otherwise noted, Scripture quotations are from the Criswell Study Bible, King James Version of the Bible.

Library of Congress Cataloging in Publication Data

Patterson, Paige.
    Pilgrim priesthood.

    Includes bibliographies.
    1. Bible. N.T. Peter, 1st—Commentaries. I. Bible.
N.T. Peter, 1st. II. Title.
BS2795.3.P37 1982   227'.92077   82-14510
ISBN 0-8407-5827-8

Twenty-five years of ministry, beginning as a fifteen-year-old boy, have brought all the trials and tribulations that one might expect, and many more triumphs and joys than I ever deserved. Since the beginning, when she was just a cherished friend, and increasingly across the years, my constant confidant, companion, and source of earthly inspiration has been a remarkably unselfish woman of prayer and faith after the order of Hannah, Ruth, Esther, the virtuous woman of Proverbs 31, Mary, and Priscilla. To my wife, Dorothy, the gift of God as the Greek name specifies, I dedicate this commentary on First Peter. In a real sense it is hers as much as it is mine. As Proverbs 31:28 promises, "Her children arise up, and call her blessed; her husband also, and he praiseth her."

C O N T E N T S

About the Author

Paige Patterson is Associate Pastor of First Baptist Church in Dallas and President of the Criswell Center for Biblical Studies. He received his B.A. from Hardin-Simmons University in Abilene, Texas, and his Th.M. and Th.D. from New Orleans Baptist Theological Seminary in Louisiana.

In addition to *A Pilgrim Priesthood: An Exposition of 1 Peter,* Patterson has written *Living in Hope of Eternal Life: An Exposition of Titus; The Great Commission, Act III;* and "The Issue Is Truth," "The Priesthood of the Believer," and "Strange Fire in the Holy of Holies" in the *Shophar Papers.* He served as Managing Editor of the Criswell Study Bible published by Nelson in 1979.

Patterson is a member of the advisory and/or governing boards of the American Association for Jewish Evangelism, the Evangelical Theological Society, the Near East Archaeological Society, the Hawaii Baptist Academy, the International Council on Biblical Inerrancy, the Religious Rountable, and the National Council on Policy.

He is a panelist for American Religious Town Hall television broadcast, a preacher on the Criswell Hour radio broadcast, and is listed in *Who's Who in Religion* and *Men of Achievement.*

P R E F A C E

The fast pace and sociological upheaval of modernity create a climate in which the succinct message of First Peter is, if anything, as valuable to Christians today as it was to the original recipients. The emphasis of the epistle on the pilgrim posture stresses the distinctiveness of the Christian lifestyle and the allegiance of the saints to a city "whose builder and maker is God." But Christian pilgrims are not "just a passin' through" as the song indicates. They constitute a "pilgrim priesthood" on a royal mission, men and women whose loving responses to suffering and hardship will constitute irrefutable proof of a regenerating experience with the Creator-Redeemer of this world.

This volume is an attempt to present an exposition of First Peter in the light of the current intellectual, sociological, and theological milieu. Hopefully the purpose of the author to prepare a commentary which would not only meet the needs of the layman but also provide insights for pastors and other scholars has been realized to some extent. Keeping in mind the English reader who is not a student of Greek, I have labored extensively in word studies and etymologies in a style approximating that of Spiros Zodhiates' commentary on James or Kenneth Wuest's volumes on numerous New Testament books.

The author is aware of James Barr's critique of the *Theological*

Dictionary of the New Testament. In *Semantics of Biblical Language,* Barr argues that words do not draw their major significance from etymology but rather from context. While this insight is true, the relative number of scholars and other Bible students who have read Barr on the one hand versus the *Theological Dictionary,* Wuest, or Zodhiates on the other, suggests the obvious. One must begin with some sort of meaning in a word before he can ascertain how, if at all, the context has altered or shaded the original sense of the word. I have tried not to be oblivious to contextual, temporal, sociological, and other interpretive factors, while at the same time devoting considerable attention to the words of the text and the significance captured in each.

Occasional illustrative material occurs, a practice generally considered passé in expositional commentaries. My defense for such practice is embodied in the following lines:

> Truth in closest words shall fail,
> When truth embodied in a tale
> Shall enter in at lowly doors.

The best of the critical commentaries on First Peter remain the works of E. G. Selwyn, *The First Epistle of St. Peter,* and Charles Bigg, *A Critical and Exegetical Commentary on the Epistles of St. Peter and St. Jude* in the *International Critical Commentary.* My indebtedness to these and to a host of other excellent treatises on First Peter will be apparent in the body of the text and certainly in the footnotes. I am also indebted to a loyal, faithful team of assistants—my executive assistant, Martha Seaton, and my three student assistants, Barrett Duke, Michael Wiechmann, and Salvatore Sberna, all superb young preachers, for helping me with a multitude of tasks. My gratitude also to Dr. Roy Metts, professor of New Testament and Greek at the Criswell Center, for his valuable insights and counsel. Above all, my gratitude should be expressed to my daughter Carmen, who is my home librarian, my son Armour, who is my assistant in physical fitness, and my wife, Dorothy, chief archivist and inspiration for the whole Patterson and Kelley clans.

President's Suite
Criswell Center for Biblical Studies

The year was A.D. 65. Nero Claudius Caesar had ascended the throne only eleven years earlier. What began as a peaceful reign had swiftly degenerated into a bloodbath. Nero first plotted the murder of his own mother Agrippina. Furthermore, the playboy Roman emperor was suspected of setting fire to a portion of the city located on the Esquiline hill, on which he anticipated the erection of his fabulous Golden Palace. Nero found in the Christian minority of Rome an ideal scapegoat. Almost every zealous expression of evangelical Christianity has had much to say about ultimate realities. Early Christians warned of an approaching day when the "elements would melt with fervent heat." They spoke of God as "a consuming fire." Such an "incendiary fellowship" provided Nero an ideal prey to saddle with the blame.

The ensuing persecution was probably local only in its extension. But the significance of the event must be reckoned in terms of the precedent it established. Other than a brief upheaval directed generally at Jews during the reign of Claudius, this was the first of many persecutions directed against Christianity by the State. Already Christians were suffering from the hatred of unbelieving Jews. In addition, the pressures and trials of daily life confronted the Christian, who had an essentially optimistic commitment in spite of his talk about judgment.

How were the followers of Jesus to evaluate the fiery trials through which they were passing? Such a question has been voiced by Christians in every age. For such inquiries, First Peter continues to speak God's peace and to promise certain victory. To embattled Christians today behind iron and bamboo curtains, the words of the Holy Spirit, who moved the fisherman to write, are like a sparkling oasis amid the desert of suffering. And who is able to discern the moment when the burden of trial or tragedy may hang heavily upon any one of us? First Peter is God's revelation to the Christian who, in any day, must find his way home through the dark valley of suffering.

The first essential for successfully countering persecution is to recognize that this world, which "is no friend to grace," is not the final destiny. Hence believers are pilgrims, sojourners in the land. But they are nonetheless pilgrims with a purpose. As a royal priesthood, they are the Redeemer's envoys sent to proclaim the message of salvation.

Author

The authorship of First Peter, like most of the New Testament books, has been the subject of debate among the critics. But among conservative scholars, there is unanimity that the traditional arguments for Petrine authorship are more than adequate to establish Peter as the author. J. H. A. Hart, certainly no fundamentalist, has written in the *Expositor's Greek Testament* that the critics'

. . . reasons are chiefly interesting as symptoms of presuppositions inherited from past controversies. They reveal (for example) a tendency to resent the attribution of divine authority to the apostles, and a tendency—which others share—to ignore the relatively mature theology to which, as a matter of fact, the first Christian missionaries were bred before ever they became missionaries or Christians at all.[1]

---

[1] J. H. A. Hart, *The First Epistle General of Peter* in *The Expositor's Greek Testament*, vol. V, p. 8.

Some have maintained that Silvanus was the amanuensis (secretary) for the letter. They maintain that the message is Peter's but that the penning of the letter was done by Silvanus, who, according to this view, was more skillful in Greek than was Peter. This view is based on 5:12 (see discussion there), which identifies Silvanus as a participant in some respect in the epistle. This view does no harm to the basic thesis that the letter is essentially that of Simon Peter.

Adolf von Harnack, noted historian of dogma, though certainly not conservative in his theological posture, doubted that a "Pseudo-Peter" wrote the present "fragment." Major arguments against Petrine authorship have always been: (1) that the epistle has too much ostensible indebtedness to Paul, (2) that it contains no reminiscences of the life and doctrine of Jesus, (3) that the Greek is more advanced than what could be expected of a Galilean peasant, (4) that the epistle reflects conditions which Peter did not live to see, and (5) that according to 5:12 Silvanus was probably the author.[2]

The first objection is easily dismissed by simply noting that a core of Christian ideas and expressions might be expected to develop on a common front. Besides, Paul's ideas had, by the time of the writing of First Peter, already begun to be widely disseminated. Furthermore, there are more differences from Paul's style and approach than there are similarities.

The second objection to Petrine authorship is simply a matter of pandering assumptions. Why must a small pastoral letter necessarily contain references to the life of Christ? This objection is really nothing but an argument from silence, which is always weak at best.

The third objection fails on similar grounds. How are we to know that Peter would not have acquired facility, perhaps even remarkable facility, in Greek? Lack of formal training in early years does not affect intellectual potential. Living in a Greek-speaking community would be sufficient for an adept mind to grasp wide communicative skills.

---

[2]*Ibid*, p. 9.

The fourth objection to Peter's authorship, once again, is theory based on a presupposition that the basic ecclesiology reflected in 5:1-4 could not have developed very early in the first century. But how can this presupposition be tested? Furthermore, why is it impossible that God could have revealed His ecclesiological purposes to the early church? The fact is that this objection is still another theory which developed out of a rationalistic tendency to reject the authority of the Bible.

The fifth objection would be tenable if it could be determined exactly what is meant by "through Silvanus" in 5:12 (see discussion of 5:12). But certainty about the meaning of the phrase eludes the student, and most scholars of evangelical persuasion recognize that it is unlikely that the words mean any more than that Silvanus was a recording amanuensis. Perhaps he was only the courier to deliver the epistle.

Furthermore, early evidences abound for acknowledging the hand of Peter. Irenaeus, bishop of Lyon, was a protégé of Polycarp, who was bishop of Smyrna and friend of the beloved disciple John. Irenaeus avows that the epistle was penned by Simon, son of John, to whom Jesus had given the name Cephas. He says in a matter-of-fact way, "Peter says in his Epistle . . ." and then quotes First Peter 1:8.[3] This witness is very early, certainly prior to A.D. 200. Other quotations from and allusions to First Peter are found in *The Epistle of Barnabas, The Shepherd of Hermas, The Epistle to Diognetus,* Justin Martyr, and Theophilus of Antioch. Eusebius, fourth-century church historian, has a passage in which he acknowledges the authenticity of Petrine authorship of First Peter, though he calls into question Second Peter. Eusebius comments that the "ancient elders" used First Peter freely in their own writings as an undisputed work.[4]

---

[3]Alexander Roberts and James Donaldson, *The Ante-Nicene Fathers,* vol. I, p. 472.

[4]Philip Schaff and Henry Wace, *A Select Library of Nicene and Post-Nicene Fathers of the Christian Church,* Second Series, vol. I, p. 133.

With this evidence I shall proceed in accepting Peter as the human author. A fisherman of Bethsaida by profession, Simon, the son of John, was nicknamed *Cephas* (meaning "stone" in Aramaic) by Jesus. Translated into Greek, the name was *Petros* or Peter. He had at least one brother, Andrew, who was also a member of the original twelve. Matthew 8:14 tells us of the mother of Peter's wife. First Corinthians 9:5 seems to provide evidence that Peter's wife labored by his side in the missionary travels. The reference to Marcus as the son of the author (5:13) is probably a reference to John Mark who was possibly led to Christ by Simon Peter or who was at least a careful pupil of the fisherman. The sonship is spiritual rather than biological.

Peter was the most prominent member of the twelve Christ chose. His importance in the early church is abundantly witnessed through the first fifteen chapters of Acts. Then he abruptly disappears from the sacred record. He is mentioned five times in Galatians. Other than the two epistles which bear his name, together with the references in Galatians, Acts 15 closes the story of Peter.

Curiosity demands to know what happened to such a towering personality. Why does one so immersed in honor just vanish from our New Testament? In answer to that question it must be remembered that the only person the New Testament seeks to magnify is Jesus. The Holy Spirit directed the writing of historical material essential to Christian knowledge for the perpetuity of the Lord's Church. The deeds of men are recorded not to satisfy our curiosity but to teach us God's will and purposes.

Tradition says that Peter was martyred in Rome. History neither affirms nor denies this. It is certainly possible that Peter died in Rome under Nero. There is no convincing evidence that Peter was ever bishop of Rome or that he had anything to do with the establishment of the original Roman congregation, much less the later development in Rome known as Catholicism. We are not wrong to exercise our minds in an effort to determine extra-biblical facts about Peter. But when we speak authoritatively, we must stop with Acts (see discussion on 5:13).

Recipients

The recipients of the letter are identified in verse 1, to which we will give attention later. This epistle was evidently intended to be a circular letter addressed to both Hebrew and Gentile Christians in Asia Minor who were beginning to encounter the heavy hand of opposition in isolated pockets, and even to suffer some at the hands of local authorities.

The specific areas designated in 1:1 are Pontus, Galatia, Cappadocia, Asia, and Bithynia. Two of these areas, Pontus and Cappadocia, are mentioned as part of Paul's missionary enterprise. Paul had attempted to enter Bithynia but was disallowed by the Holy Spirit. Galatia and Asia are places where Paul did labor. However, both designations are somewhat ambiguous. Furthermore, Peter probably has reference to the northern portion of those provinces where the work of Paul had not been extensive.

Pontus was a region of Asia Minor (modern Turkey) which occupied the southern coast of the Euxine or Black Sea. The area is mountainous but fertile with a good climate. The region is sufficiently remote that neither Greek nor Roman culture thoroughly permeated it. Immediately south of Pontus was Cappadocia. Fruits and cereals are products of the area though the chief support derived from pastoral interests. In the two regions combined, there was no significant density of population. Rural life dominated.

Bithynia lay to the west of the other territories mentioned with the exception of Asia. In the north it was fronted by the Black Sea, while on the west it guarded the strategic Bosporus. Asia was the region immediately south of Bithynia. This area was the area of the seven cities of Asia addressed by John in the Apocalypse. But the northern regions were not so heavily populated. Galatia lay to the east of Asia, south of Pontus. The northern fringe of this elongated territory was the home of the ancient Celtic peoples. Again the most populous areas of Galatia were those to which Paul ministered in such cities as Lystra, Derbe, and Iconium.

The general pattern which is apparent here is that Paul, the cosmopolitan Roman, pressed the work of the kingdom in the cities, while Peter, the Galilean fisherman and outdoorsman, labored in areas more remote but still important. This cooperation was apparently not a planned strategy mapped out in apostolic convention. It is positive testimony to the guiding hand of the Holy Spirit in early missionary expansion.

Origin

The epistle purports to have been written in Babylon (see discussion in 5:12). Which Babylon intended is not so easily determined. "Babylon" is used in the Apocalypse as a cryptogram for "Rome." But First Peter is not decidedly apocalyptic literature. Strong tradition suggests that Peter labored in Asia Minor before going to Rome where he was executed by crucifixion, upside down. When Paul wrote to the church at Rome around A.D. 58, he greets a host of people, but Peter is not among them. Again the Prison Epistles written from Rome make no mention of Peter's presence, suggesting that the celebrated and acknowledged leader surely was not present.

Of course, all of this simply may have preceded Peter's own journey to Rome. But equally plausible would be the hypothesis that just as the two apostles divided their labors in Asia Minor, so also they parted, with Paul going to the urbanized west while Peter departed for the more rural east, settling finally in Babylon of Mesopotamia from which he writes. If so, then a church is in existence in Babylon by the sixth decade of the first century. Modern confusion reigns, but the original readers doubtless knew of Peter's whereabouts and greeted his communication with gladness of heart.

O   N   E

The Proliferation of Grace

Author's Translation (1:1-12)

1—Peter, an apostle of Jesus Christ, to the elect pilgrims of the dispersion in Pontus, Galatia, Cappadocia, Asia, and Bithynia,

2—According to the foreknowledge of God the Father, through the sanctification of the Spirit, into submissiveness and the sprinkling of the blood of Jesus Christ; grace to you and peace be steadily increased.

3—Praised be the God and Father of our Lord Jesus Christ, who as a result of his abundant mercy has caused us to be born anew into a living hope by means of the resurrection of Jesus Christ out of the dead,

4—Unto an inheritance imperishable, and unstained, and unfading, reserved in the heavens for us,

5—Who are being continually kept by the power of God through faith unto salvation ready to be unveiled in the last time.

6—In which you keep on rejoicing [even] if the suffering of various trials is necessary for the present, short time,

7—So that the test of your faith, [being] more honored than gold which is being [destroyed], moreover having been examined through fire, may be found resulting in abundant praise and glory and honor at the unveiling of Jesus Christ,

8—Whom not having seen, you continually love, in whom,

[though] not presently beholding, you are trusting, yes, continually rejoicing with joy unspeakable, and having been filled with glory,

9—Perpetually receiving the fulfillment of your faith, the salvation of [your] souls:

10—Concerning which salvation prophets, who were prophesying concerning the grace [provided] for you, sought out and searched thoroughly,

11—Continually investigating [to determine] what time or what kind of time the Spirit of Christ was making evident to them, bearing witness prior to the sufferings of Christ and the glory which followed,

12—To whom it was revealed that, not to themselves, but to you they were ministering the same things which were recently proclaimed to you through those who evangelized you, and by the Holy Spirit who was sent from Heaven; into which things angels are ardently desiring to look.

The Plan of Salvation (1:1-2)*

1—Peter, an apostle of Jesus Christ, to the strangers scattered throughout Pontus, Galatia, Cappadocia, Asia, and Bithynia,

2—Elect according to the foreknowledge of God the Father, through sanctification of the Spirit, unto obedience and sprinkling of the blood of Jesus Christ: Grace unto you, and peace, be multiplied.

Verse 1. Men of antiquity assumed the recipient of a letter to be the intended reader. The crucial question then became the identification of the author. Accordingly, Peter affixed his signature to the letter, signaling its source even before he addressed those for whom it was planned. By A.D. 63 the name "Peter" was intimately known by every community of believers. The rich pericopes of the gospel had already been told wherever Jesus was preached. One or more of the Gospels had probably not only been written but also widely circulated. Hence, Peter states only his name with one

*Scripture passages used after the Author's Translation and throughout the text are from the Criswell Study Bible, King James Version.

qualifying phrase to describe himself—"an apostle of Jesus Christ." The phrase is not necessary to establish his identity. Rather, the phrase is marshalled by Peter to affirm his authority. This is not merely a friendly letter from a beloved brother. It is an epistle from one who speaks with apostolic authority.

Requirements for apostleship are reasonably specific in the New Testament documents. Four distinct features of apostleship are discernible (see Acts 1:21-24 and 1 Cor. 12:28).

(1) An apostle must have been in the company of the followers of Jesus from the Lord's baptism at the hands of John until His ascension (Acts 1:21-22).

(2) An apostle also must have been an eyewitness of the resurrected Christ (Acts 1:22).

(3) An apostle had to be specifically chosen of God for this assignment (Acts 1:24).

(4) An apostle had to be given the gift *(charisma)* of apostleship (1 Cor. 12:28).

Paul speaks of his apostleship as though his was an exceptional case (see 1 Cor. 15:8), perhaps due to his inability to meet the initial criterion. But Peter, the author of this epistle, meets all of the criteria and identifies himself as an apostle. Two other features of apostleship merit attention. Obviously some of the spiritual gifts *(pneumatika)* or grace gifts *(charismata)* are not intended to be perpetuated throughout the church age. Since no one today can meet either of the first two essentials, one must conclude that the gift of apostleship was temporary. The same might also be true for other gifts. The importance of this limitation upon apostleship is Peter's focus in his second epistle (1:12-21). Realizing the inevitability of his own "decease" *(exodos)*, Peter, as an eyewitness (2 Peter 1:16), desires to leave behind an authoritative account of these events so that his congregations (1) will remember these things after there is no apostle (2 Peter 1:15) and (2) will be established in "present truth" (2 Peter 1:12).

The meaning of the word "apostle" further magnifies this

unique office. The compound Greek word is comprised of *stellō*, to send, and *apo*, a preposition meaning "from." In other words, an apostle is one whose authority is derived from a commission of God. The apostle is sent from God with the message upon which the church is to be built (Eph. 2:20). Therefore, Peter's message is not his own. He writes as an apostle of Jesus Christ.

The recipients are next identified as the elect pilgrims of the dispersion. The word "pilgrims" *(parepidēmois)* means "beside the people." It is a precise term for defining the relationship of the believer to the world in which he dwells. Scripture demands: "come out from among them, and be ye separate" (2 Cor. 6:17). The word translated "separate" means "to establish a border between." Jesus, on the other hand, speaks of Christians as the salt of the earth and the light of the world. The answer to this apparent paradox is observed in the pilgrim nature of the Christian life. The position of the Christian is beside the people. This achieves both the necessary separation (out from *among* the people) and the crucial permeation and penetration of the people through constant ministering contacts with the spiritually deficient.

The concept of the pilgrim life is important to the success of our work as spiritual catalysts. A sense of being out of place here—of belonging elsewhere—must exist. Yet an unaccomplished kingly commission binds us to continued service as ambassadors. Brother Andrew's spine-tingling autobiography entitled *God's Smuggler* provides an illustration of this type of life. As a Bible-smuggler in the heart of Warsaw, Poland, Brother Andrew found himself in the middle of a singing, shouting, clapping, Communist demonstration. He did not belong, and he feared that his facial expressions revealed his uneasiness. Yet, he could not leave because the word of God had to be disseminated.

Such must always be the pilgrim road. The distastefulness of lawlessness, the dwindling of love, the very oppressiveness of satanic forces in the world awaken in the pilgrim believer a longing for home (2 Cor. 5:8). Still, his commitment to evangelism and missions keeps him beside the people who grope in darkness and focuses his light of love upon Christ for the benefit of each slave who will reach in faith to Jesus, obtaining freedom in Him.

The pilgrim life is essentially different in terms of commitment. The man of the world is committed to himself, to hedonism, or to materialism. The pilgrim's allegiance is to Christ, to others in Christ's name, and to himself as an instrument of righteousness. He remains only loosely attached to many of the values which society regards as important. Instead he holds tightly to his Lord and to a set of values that are often consigned by a host world to a position of relative insignificance.[1]

The pilgrims who are addressed by Peter are pilgrims of the dispersion. The word dispersion *(diasporas)* is a general term employed in the first century to designate Jews living outside of Palestine. It appears that the term has a broader application here, though doubtless in Peter's mind the first group presenting themselves would be the believing Hebrews of the dispersion. As has been noted, however, the epistle allows no ethnic exclusiveness. Both believing Jews and trusting Gentiles are included. Further confirmation of this fact is given in that these pilgrims of the dispersion are limited to those who are elect pilgrims. These are those dispersed ones who have been unified in the body of Christ.

The areas designated by the apostle are broad indeed.

---

[1]A recent treatise on First Peter by John H. Elliot is billed as sociological exegesis of the epistle and focuses on the "pilgrim" emphasis as thematic. In *A Home for the Homeless,* the author argues that it is improper to see the pilgrim passages as indications of the transient nature of life on earth while preparing for an abode in heaven (p. 44). Rather Elliott sees the references as representing only behavioral options. As indicated above, behavior is involved, but it is much too narrow to confine the pilgrim language to temporal sociological factors (e.g., Heb. 11:8-10, 1 Peter 1:4-5, 3:22, 5:4). In these passages Peter and the author of Hebrews indicate that their ultimate allegiance is bound up in a "heavenly citizenship."

Charles Bigg, in the *International Critical Commentary,* sees in the enumeration of these areas evidence of a secondary missionary enterprise more extensive than any of Paul's.[2] Certainly the audiences destined to listen to this letter were scattered over a considerable portion of Asia Minor. Pontus was located in northern Asia Minor near the Black Sea, bordered on the east by lesser Armenia, on the west by Galatia, and on the south by Cappadocia. The Galatian province in central Asia Minor was also the designated recipient of Paul's correspondence. Cappadocia was to the south of Pontus and east of Galatia. Bithynia was north of Galatia, immediately adjacent to the Black Sea. Exactly what Asia is intended to include is not clear. It could be a very broad designation including the rest of Asia Minor, but this would be unlikely since it occurs in a list of specified provinces. Perhaps it refers to the areas known as Mysia, Lydia, and Asian Phrygia. If so, it harmonizes with other evidences pointing to a keen interest on the part of Peter in northern Asia Minor. This leaves southern Asia Minor to Paul and his associates. John is later highly influential in western Asia Minor.

Verse 2. Having identified the recipients *geographically,* Peter now identifies them *theologically.* They are the elect according to the foreknowledge of God the Father. The doctrine of election has long been a battleground among evangelical Christians. Amid the confusion precipitated in such discussions, one professor compared the doctrine to a turnstile in a grocery store: "It is a lot of trouble to everyone, but it will not keep anyone out." It might be added that the doctrine of election, like the turnstyle, serves notice that we gain entrance at the invitation and timing of the owner, in this case, God.

Actually, much of the confusion about election might have been avoided had students of the Bible remembered that

---

[2]Charles Bigg, *A Critical and Exegetical Commentary on the Epistles of St. Peter and St. Jude* in the *International Critical Commentary,* p. 69.

"God's thoughts are not our thoughts." God has revealed much to us, but the immensity of God precludes anything approximating full knowledge of God. Rather than attempting to resolve the apparent paradox created by the twin biblical avowals of the sovereignty of God and the freedom of man, why not preach both and ask instead a question which has a plausible solution: Why is the doctrine of election given in Scripture? There are four answers which are provided to that query in Romans 8.

(1) The doctrine of election establishes salvation as an act of God from beginning to end, eliminating human works altogether in the pursuit of salvation (see Rom. 8:30).

(2) The doctrine of election assures us the impossibility of apostasy or falling from salvation. How could one of God's elect fall (see Rom. 8:35)?

(3) The doctrine of election promises us the providential intervention of God in behalf of His children (see Rom. 8:28).

(4) The doctrine of election assures us that God's hand rests upon the nations of the world, guiding history to the climax which God has determined for it (see Rom. 8:21-22).

This does not imply that it is off limits to theologize about the relationships which exist between God's electing sovereignty on one hand and man's freedom and responsibility to choose on the other.

In a magnificent trinitarian construction, the passage before us declares the activities of the persons of the Godhead in the redemptive plan. We were elected in accordance with God's foreknowledge, and we were set apart unto God the Father by the Holy Spirit on the basis of our submissiveness to the finished blood atonement of Jesus Christ, God's son. That this election is according to God's foreknowledge is declared both here and by Paul in Romans 8:29.

Some men have argued that since God's decree cannot be said to be chronologically later than His omniscience, it is, therefore, simultaneous with His omniscience. Yet, if Romans 8 is handled this way consistently, then our calling, justification, and glorification must be lumped together also. This is true from God's standpoint—from eternity. Yet in time glorification, for example, obviously follows justification both logically and chronologically. Of course, God sees the consummation as perfectly as He sees the inception, and this He has done eternally.

The biblical writers under the direction of the Holy Spirit have chosen to begin with foreknowledge. The very construction of the word must be considered. The word is made up of *pro* (before) and *gnōsis* (knowledge). We derive our word "prognosticate" (meaning "the sharing of a knowledge of future events") from this compound Greek word. If this tells us nothing else, it at least assures us of the absolute justice of God and leaves the way to salvation open to every person experiencing godly sorrow unto repentance (see 2 Cor. 2:7). Furthermore, it certifies salvation as the grace of God from beginning to end. Man cannot boast.

Election is not cheap. It is not mere choice. For each man chosen by God there is a price of redemption. That price is said to be the sprinkling of the blood of Jesus Christ (see 1 Peter 1:2). "Blood" by itself might refer only to violent death, but the "sprinkling of blood" points definitely to the sacrifices.[3] The Old Testament sacrificial system provided for ceremonial cleansing by the sprinkling of sacrificial blood on men or on utensils. The sprinkling of blood on the mercy seat on the Day of Atonement was plainly pointing to a price involved in redemption and to a consequent inner cleansing. The Scripture teaches that the shedding of the blood of Christ on the cross is both the price of redemption and the provision for regeneration. Some people ridicule such a vicarious substitutionary atonement. Nevertheless, Colossians 1:20 speaks of Jesus as "having made peace through the blood of his cross." This is the repeated declaration of the Bible. Christ's atonement abolishes the sin-constructed enmity between God and

---

[3]Leon Morris, *The Cross in the New Testament*, p. 321.

man. The price for man's reconciliation to God has now been paid.

But the electing grace of God and the purchase of that elected one by Christ must be appropriated by the individual. Salvation is the work of God alone, but the heart of the sinner must be receptive. This act of repentance and faith is submission to the cleansing provided by Christ. The word translated submissiveness is *hupakoēn* which derives from *hupo* (under) and *akouō* (to hear). It indicates that one is so persuaded of the truth of that which he hears that he subjects himself to it or comes under it. If a man is persuaded of God's electing love for him and of the efficacy of Christ's atonement in his behalf, he submits in faith to Jesus and thereby appropriates that sacrifice to meet his own need.

When this commitment is made, the Holy Spirit activates His ministry of regeneration. He also sanctifies the believer. The word "sanctify" is *hagiasmō* from the root *hagios,* meaning "set apart" or "holy." The Holy Spirit makes the believer holy or sets him apart from the rest of the world to belong to God. This is positional sanctification. Scripture also knows of the process of progressive sanctification or growing "set-apartness" to God.

The result of God's grace in our lives is the proliferation of peace. Thus, the salutation closes with a prayer for the grace of the triune God and a hope that peace will be steadily increased. In the Greek New Testament, that phrase translated "peace be steadily increased" is just two words, *eirēnē plēthunthein.* The last word is a relatively rare optative mood in the Greek Testament. A. T. Robertson remarks that the optative in Greek is really ill-named, since it is more than a mere wish.[4] The optative mood in Greek is used whenever a certain action or condition is deemed to be possible without reference to (in this case, regardless of) the existing conditions.

---

[4]A. T. Robertson, *A Grammar of the Greek New Testament in the Light of Historical Research,* p. 325.

Peter's use of the optative mood in this expression of peace sets the tone for the whole book and is, therefore, of great import. The existing conditions are those of pressing hardship. Regardless of the stresses around the believer, he may look for the steady increase of inner peace and calm in his own life. Gideon had grasped that truth firmly when in Judges 6, amid rumblings of Midianite power, he constructed an altar in Ophrah and called it Jehovah-shalom ("Jehovah is peace"). To be the recipient of God's grace is to know an ever increasing amount of God's peace.

A concluding word is needed concerning the trinitarian affirmation of Simon Peter. Salvation resides in God alone. That Peter accepted Jesus as God and the Holy Spirit as God is clear since each is credited with a significant aspect of salvation. Though the word "trinity" does not occur in Scripture, the reality of the triune God could scarcely be made more explicit. Here you have relationships existing within the Trinity, separation of tasks and procedures according to the three Persons, yet full unity of purpose and accomplishment as found in the one divine nature.

The Fullness of Salvation (1:3-5)

3—Blessed be the God and Father of our Lord Jesus Christ, which according to his abundant mercy hath begotten us again unto a lively hope by the resurrection of Jesus Christ from the dead,

4—To an inheritance incorruptible, and undefiled, and that fadeth not away, reserved in heaven for you.

5—Who are kept by the power of God through faith unto salvation ready to be revealed in the last time.

Verse 3. In the Beatitudes, various groups are said to be "blessed." But the word which is translated "blessed" in the King James Version is a different word with a meaning so readily distinctive that "praised" is a better translation. In the Beatitudes, as well as in numerous other passages, the word "blessed" is *makarios,* which the Amplified Bible properly expands to include the concepts "happy" and "to be envied." It is a word used often in Scripture but always in reference to the condition of a man who is rightly related to God.

Eulogētos, the word in First Peter 1:3, is used only of the righteous man's response to the God through whose grace he is made to be *makarios* or happy. It derives from *eu* (well) and *logos* (word). The word gives us our English word "eulogy," which refers to comments of praise usually delivered in honor of the deceased at a funeral. Thus to praise or bless God is to utter good words concerning Him because of who He is (God and Father) and what He has done (caused men to be born anew).

The ability to praise God is something of a lost art. Many speak lightly of God, but few give audible praise to Him. A deacon in one of my pastorates sometimes astonished people with the zeal of his public prayer. But I loved to hear him talk to the Lord because he said wonderfully sweet things to Jesus and demonstrated genuine appreciation for the grace relationship which he possesses. This is the meaning of Peter's exhortation. He wants Christians to say something publicly about Jesus. Furthermore, we are to speak to Him so as to identify clearly the position Jesus holds in our lives.

Peter's mention of the Son of God in His threefold name, Lord Jesus Christ, betrays the awe which the apostle felt concerning Jesus. To begin in reverse, "Christ" means "the anointed one" and is equivalent to the Hebrew term "Messiah." In reality it is a title, not a name. Jesus is His personal name and denotes the purpose of the incarnation. His name is the same as "Joshua" or "Hosea" in the Old Testament and means "Jehovah is salvation." "Lord" is a title of acknowledgment. The word is the translation of *kurios,* meaning "master." Peter's use of the term spells out his own relationship to Jesus the Christ as Lord.

As has been said, a portion of this praise is due to God because of the new birth which is available to all. Three things are evident concerning the new birth: (1) It is brought about by the Father as a result of His great mercy; (2) it provides for a living hope; and (3) it is accomplished as a result of Christ's conquering of death in His resurrection. "Born anew" is a translation of *anagennēsas*, which is a compound of *ana* (again) and *gennaō* (to be born).

The emphasis of the New Testament is upon a new start—a completely new life. That life is a gift which is secured by no religious attainment of man's but by Christ's atonement. The living hope of spiritual life's replacing spiritual death is secured by the resurrection of Jesus "from the dead," as the King James Version translates that phrase. The author uses the preposition *ek*, meaning "out of." God removed His Son from the sphere and power of death. That miracle paves the way for a similar feat for the disciple. This deliverance begins in spiritual birth and reaches its consummation in bodily resurrection.

In the Greek Testament the word which has been rendered "caused us to be born anew," is an aorist tense participle. The aorist tense is used here to indicate an act viewed in its entirety, from the viewpoint of its existing results. Physical birth is preceded by a period of preparation and followed by years of growth, yet the actual birth is a single event. A time of witness or influences of circumstance may prepare a man for the new birth. But the new or spiritual birth, like its physical counterpart, is a revolutionary event that takes place at a given time and is complete within itself. Certainly man should grow as a Christian, but one grows into maturity, not into life. Man cannot grow into salvation, but having been born of God, he may grow into spiritual adulthood.

Peter says that we are born anew into a living hope. The use of the word "hope" is not intended to foster doubts in the mind of anyone concerning the certainty of the message of Peter. The German New Testament scholar Rudolf Bultmann is mistaken in finding in Scripture only a kernel of truth, which must be extracted from its mythological trappings, but he is frequently correct in his evaluation of what the primitive

Christians thought and believed. Writing of hope as used in first-century Christian vocabulary, he says, "It embraces at once the three elements of expectation and the future, trust, and patience in waiting."[5] Hope for the early believer was the opposite of fear of the future. "To have hope," says Bultmann, "is a sign that things are well with us." Our "hope" for final redemption does not refer to something which may or may not develop. When we say that we have a living hope, we indicate our confidence in the future, our consistent trust in Jesus to provide salvation, and our patient endurance in the race to which we are presently assigned. This is Christian hope!

Verse 4. More than a living hope is obtained for the believer in the realization of God's redemptive plan. Men are born into a status of heirship. This inheritance is described as imperishable, unstained, and unfading—three negative terms. In his superb commentary on First Peter, F. B. Meyer notes that,

It is so much easier to say what the inheritance is not, than to set down the elements of its exceeding weight of glory.[6]

We must content ourselves with saying mostly what heaven is not because "Eye hath not seen, nor ear heard, neither have entered into the heart of man, the things which God hath prepared for them that love him" (1 Cor. 2:9). Three affirmations about the inheritance of the saints are specified. The inheritance is (1) imperishable in its substance, (2) unstained in its purity, and (3) unfading in its beauty. Every earthly thing we know suffers weakness at one or more of these points. Everything either perishes, fades in its beauty, or is invaded by elements which contaminate its purity.

Consider especially man. With age, the beauty of youth

---

[5]Gerhard Kittel, ed., *Theological Dictionary of the New Testament,* vol. II, p. 531.

[6]F. B. Meyer, *Tried by Fire: Expositions of the First Epistle of Peter,* p. 15.

fades away, muscles sag, skin wrinkles, and energy diminishes. Long before this, man has lost his moral and spiritual purity by playing the deadly game of sin. Finally, his physical body perishes altogether in the sleep of death. What is true of man is heightened in every experience and every material benefit of life. Material possessions lose their luster and fade until they perish. Only that which God has imparted to us, which Scripture terms the earnest or the first and guarantee payment of the Spirit, abides eternally.

Better still, the beauty of that inheritance increases, its substance multiplies, and its purity is eternally secured by God. I grew up in Texas where football probably is second only to God. As a boy, it seemed to me that the greatest experiences of my life were those days spent as quarterback on a winning team. The passing of years has changed all that. The further removed from boyhood I am, the more glorious becomes the one thing that now stands out in my mind—the experience of giving my heart to Christ. Second to that, those first successful youthful attempts at witnessing for my Lord are burned into my memory. In short, experience has underscored the truth of what Jesus long ago said concerning the abiding value of heavenly treasure.

Finally, the Lord promises that this treasure is reserved in the heavens for us. The word reserved may also be translated "guarded." It is a military term which points to the certainty of the inheritance. The vault for this treasure is said to be in the heavens. Much has been said concerning the supposed conviction of scriptural writers that they were living in a three-storied universe. Actually, the cellar and upper story are clearly spiritual realms in Scripture. That more knowledge of our universe was available to the inspired writers than usually is granted them may be observed in Isaiah's statement about God as the one who "sitteth upon the circle of the earth" (Is. 40:22).

It is very evident in Scripture that the writers knew of three heavens: the firmament is the atmospheric heaven; the stellar or intergalactic heavens comprise the entire universe; the third realm, the heaven of heavens, is God's heaven. It is the dwelling place of the righteous and the vault where our inheritance is preserved. Even in a day of space travel to the moon and planets of our own solar system, the vastness of the stellar heavens continues to constitute an enigma to man and remains, to a large extent, inaccessible to him. Heaven, therefore, is an appropriate designation for God's dwelling. The fullness of its reality eludes man, and it is accessible only to those who die in the Lord Jesus.

Verse 5. The beauty of the inheritance is of little value if the heirs may not inherit it. Peter maintains that the heirs, like the inheritance, are kept by the power of God. We have translated the word *phrouroumenous* "continually being kept." It is a present participle, indicating continuing action. A man's salvation is continually mediated by the Lord. The word itself is one which was employed in classical Greek for the watch kept on a ship at sea and for the careful guarding of precious jewels.

The same word is used by Paul in Philippians 4:7 when the apostle promises that the peace of God "shall keep your hearts and minds through Jesus Christ." It is the power *(dunamis)* of God which continues. It is well known that our word "dynamite" comes from *dunamis.* Since dynamite is basically destructive, the word "dynamic" is probably a better comparison. The word has reference to power in the sense of the ability necessary to see a matter to its fruition.

A theologian recently argued in favor of the possibility of apostasy. Toward the end of a seventeen-page discussion of the doctrine, he concluded that three items stand out in an exposition of Hebrews:

> (1) it is possible to press on to maturity and full assurance (6:1, 11; 10:22); (2) it is possible for believers who do not press on to maturity to commit apostasy; and (3) there is no remedy for the sin of apostasy.[7]

---

[7]Dale Moody, *The Word of Truth,* p. 355.

The author of those words is to be commended for his recognition of the third point. Most advocates of the doctrine of apostasy also argue in the face of clear evidence to the contrary that one can be saved, then lost, then saved again. Hebrews 6:4-6 lucidly states that if one could forfeit his salvation (and he cannot), he could never be restored again. Most who espouse the possibility of apostasy have never entertained thoughts about how repugnant such teachings must be to God.

For example, if men are saved by grace, as Ephesians 2:8-9 and Titus 3:5 surely indicate, yet a man may lose his salvation through some rebellious act, then it follows that the impetus for retaining his salvation resides with him. Hence God may save him initially; but if he stays saved, he does so because he behaves in all matters of real spiritual consequence. It then becomes an inescapable conclusion that at least in its ultimate expression salvation is the product of the grace of God and the works of men. If it be objected that God is able to keep us from falling (see Jude 24), then why would He do that for some and not for all?

The fact is that if left to ourselves we would all apostatize. Thus our verse in First Peter affirms that we are continually kept by the power of God. For the same reason Paul rejoiced in his assurance based on the keeping power of our Lord (see 2 Tim. 1:12). This keeping aspect of salvation is only one of a number of evidences for the security of the believer and the permanency of salvation. Consider the following:

(1) The nature of salvation as regeneration (see John 3:5; Titus 3:5).

(2) The baptism of every believer into the body of Christ at conversion (see 1 Cor. 12:13).

(3) The sealing ministry of the Holy Spirit (see Eph. 4:30).

(4) The death of the believer to sin, rendering it no longer possible for him perpetually to live in sin (see Rom. 6:1-2).

(5) The renewing ministry of the Holy Spirit (see Titus 3:5).

Actually the doctrine which proposes the possibility of

apostasy falls under the censure of both Romans and Galatians because human works are added to the work of Christ as a part of the saving process. As such, the doctrine detracts from the total sufficiency of Christ's atonement on the cross as a complete remedy for sin. No wonder Peter rejoices with all believers who are kept by the power of God.

The keeping power of God is appropriated by the individual through faith. The word "faith" is *pistis*. This Greek word derives from an old Sanskrit word *pith*, which means "to become one with." *Pistis* has a general sense of trust or commitment. Therefore, the word "faith" has reference to so thorough a commitment of one's life to Christ as to become one with Him. Anything less is "lip faith" or "confessing faith" only and is insufficient to receive the gift of God.

This faith which is exercised is only the beginning of salvation. The consummation is set for a special time, Peter declares. The word for time is *kairos*, referring to God's chosen and special time, and it is used here in contrast to another Greek word for time, *kronos*, which is generally time as man reckons and understands it. Final salvation, which includes the before-mentioned inheritance—a glorified body and the presence of the Lord Himself—is yet to be unveiled. The word "unveiled" is the verb *apokaluptō*, which is made up of *apo* ("from" or "take from") and *kaluptō* ("to veil" or "to cover"), thus "to take away the veil or covering." It is a part of the Christian's legacy to anticipate a day of public revelation before the entire universe concerning his own righteousness through Christ and the reward that he has appropriated by faith.

The Testing of Salvation (1:6-9)

6—Wherein ye greatly rejoice, though now for a season, if need be, ye are in heaviness through manifold temptations:

7—That the trial of your faith, being much more precious than of gold that perisheth, though it be tried with fire, might be found unto praise and honor and glory at the appearing of Jesus Christ:

8—Whom having not seen, ye love; in whom, though now ye see him not, yet believing, ye rejoice with joy unspeakable and full of glory:

9—Receiving the end of your faith, even the salvation of your souls.

Peter has reminded his readers of the fullness of the gift of God in salvation. The reminder of God's graciousness serves as the prologue for Peter's discussion of the inevitability of suffering in this life. It is this latter theme which he now discusses. The recipients are informed of the certainty of human deprivation, but they are also instructed concerning the durable qualities of their faith. Finally, they are assured of a perpetual reward.

Verse 6. Discussion has raged concerning the words "in which you rejoice." The word translated "you rejoice" may be either in the indicative mood (mere statement of fact) or in the imperative mood (a command). Some have imagined that it is indicative and a reference to the final revelation of the salvation delineated in verse 5, that is, to a time when Christians will rejoice. Others consider it a command for action amid present circumstances because of the knowledge of a coming Savior.

We will do well to take it as an imperative. Because of his assurance in Christ, the Christian's responsibility is to radiate happiness and joy, even while immersed in human need. Regardless of the mood of the verb, it is in the middle voice. English can duplicate the active and passive voices of Greek, but the Greek middle voice has a distinctive emphasis. In this case, the activity of the participating subjects (suffering readers) in the verb (rejoice) is heavily emphasized. Peter knew that only men in Christ can rejoice. This is a unique liberty and responsibility.

Believers are to rejoice in the glories of salvation even when it is necessary to encounter various trials. In *The Faith of the Russian Evangelicals,* J. C. Pollock recounts the story of Ivan Rjaboshapka, a blacksmith in the village of Lubomirka in czarist Russia. Police, accompanied by the village priest, burst in upon a small group of believers in 1867. Since Ivan was the leader, he was flogged until only half-conscious. Asked later if the whipping were not exceedingly painful, he replied, "It burned, yes, it burned, but it was nothing to the fire of Jesus' love in my heart."[8] This is the joy of suffering for Christ that has characterized Christian sufferers of every age.

There are three things that Simon Peter notes concerning such trials. (1) They appear in almost unlimited variety. The trial may be a besetting sin that must be conquered. It may be a physical illness or the loss of a loved one. It may even be some event of a general catastrophic nature. Sometimes one is misunderstood by his fellow disciples, or deliberately maligned by a fellow Christian who should know better. Although Satan, a master of deceit, attempts this variety-package approach, we can rest in God's promise that no temptation is actually novel. He has a prepared way for us to evade the snare of each (see 1 Cor. 10:13).

(2) The trials are described temporally as of limited duration, "for the present short time." When I moved to New Orleans, my family received a less than regal welcome from the destructive hand of Hurricane Betsy. But even that awesome gale was followed by a day of beautiful sunshine. Furthermore, the tragic aftermath provided fertile ground out of which tall, stately, spiritual lives have blossomed. The longest trial is soon over. Even if life as a whole is viewed as a trial, James reminds us that physical life is but "a vapor, that appeareth for a little time, and then vanisheth away" (see James 4:14).

Verse 7. (3) Another reminder about trials is that afflictions possess definite eschatological purpose. Tribulations are viewed in verse 7 through the analogy of a process of gold purification. The idea is that just as gold is subjected to extreme heat to remove impurities and to produce a pure substance worthy of human praise, so also the followers of Jesus must tread the coals of tribulation fire. But there is

---

[8]J. C. Pollock, *The Faith of the Russian Evangelicals*, p. 62.

definite purpose. The product which emerges from such testing is a purged one. Traces of self-righteousness, impurities, pride—all will have been burned away, and the man of God will be fully furnished for use by the Master. The figure of a Christian as an ornament of praise is found also in 3:4, in which qualities such as a meek and quiet spirit are said to be acceptable adornment.

The eschatological result of tested faith is that the believer will be found receiving the praise, glory, and honor of the Lord at His unveiling. Primitive Christians were an eschatologically-minded group. They fully believed that the omniscience and omnipotence of God were moving history toward a sensational climax. This hope was a chiliastic hope, the central feature of which was the unveiling of the glorified Christ to reign in righteousness for a thousand years. To be able to be with the Lord and to have something to offer to the beauty of His reign ought to be now, as it was then, the heart's desire of the believing community.

Three specific words are used to characterize our reward. The first is the word "praise." It speaks of God's approval of the believer in contradistinction to His attitude toward those who will have shame because of failure to trust Jesus. The Lord promised a commendation to the faithful when He forecast a day upon which the Father would say, "Well done, thou good and faithful servant." To have the acclaim of the Savior is worth the short-term suffering of life.

The second term is "glory." This word *doxa* is an unusual word etymologically. It was discovered long ago that the Greek of the New Testament is not a special divine language but the Koine or "common" Greek of the marketplace. The word *doxa*, when transferred to the vernacular, experienced a radical change from its classical usage. Originally it meant "opinion." In the New Testament it denotes a state of being which is largely unattainable in this life but which is positively promised to each believer at the coming of the Lord. To be able to behold the glory (*kabod*, Hebrew) of

Jehovah was the desire of the Hebrew prophets. The shepherds on Bethlehem's hills saw the glory of the Lord shining around them at the announcement of Jesus' birth. The word "glory" suggests a radiant and glowing state.

The last term is "honor." It points to the exalted position which the glorified believer will receive as a reward for his faith. All three of these qualities are the natural properties of the Lord. They are to be bestowed upon the believer at the coming of Christ. The Christian's realm and state of existence is altered radically. He receives the commendation of the Lord and is lifted to a position of honor before the entire creation. The actual Greek term *timē* is often used to designate the attitude of the owner of a valued jewel. The jewel is a "precious" stone. The believer is a precious possession of the Lord.

Verse 8. The possibility of enduring tribulations victoriously is a reality based on the relationship of the believer with his Lord. It is, first of all, a relationship not based on sight. The author stresses this lack of physical sight by repeating the declaration twice. The word "see" is a translation of *horaō*, one of several Greek words for "see." *Horaō* is used because it speaks of viewing an object rather than of seeing as opposed to blindness. The object in question is Jesus. Peter first says that his readers had not seen the Lord at any time. The second affirmation of God's invisibility is in the present tense indicating that this is a continuous situation. Peter is not speaking of himself but of the Asian Christians who, even as we, trusted in Jesus without beholding Him.

Nevertheless, four things may be said concerning this sightless relationship, all of them stated against the backdrop of the previous verse which promised the ultimate unveiling of the Lord. First, though the Asian Christians had never seen the Lord, they kept on loving Christ. How can we love someone we have never seen? In First John, the apostle John pointed to a man's difficulty in loving an unseen God if he could not love a brother whose face he could behold.

When I was fourteen, my parents returned from an overseas mission with the deep conviction that the Lord was leading them to bring into our family a little Arab boy whom they had encountered in the streets of Jerusalem. They inquired concerning the willingness of us children to have a new brother, and the vote was unanimous in favor of the addition. It was a long time before Mohammed (who later renamed himself David) Towfic Amad actually arrived in America. But during those days of anxious waiting, furious exchange of letters, and patient hoping, a love for a brother I had never seen developed in my heart. On that memorable Sunday when he arrived, his reception was not that of a stranger but of a brother greatly loved. Yet, I had never seen him.

We have not yet seen Jesus. But He will be no stranger when He is presented to His bride in the splendor of heaven. Already we have learned to love Him. This word "love" places the emphasis upon a deep devotion, which prompts a gift of ourselves to Christ in return for His gift of Himself to us. The essential nature of love is made lucid by the Savior when He states that the primary commandment is to love God. If one really loves Jesus, he will not have to be coaxed into talking with Him or reading His word. No one will have to plead with the lover to share his estimate of the attributes and qualities of His love.

Of all the people I know, I prefer to converse with my wife. When I am away in revival and receive a letter from my beloved, I read it as though it were written on leaves of gold and bathed in honey. Moreover, the longer I have been away, the more avidly I search out the message of the letter, often rereading it. And speak of her? Certainly so! Now Jesus made it plain that we ought to love Him on a level surpassing earthly filial relations. If this is practiced, we will speak to Jesus frequently in order to speak well of Him to others. And the longer our presence with Him is delayed, the more often shall we search His letter, the Bible.

Second, God is also the object of our continuing trust. Trust is again that same word *pistis* and derives naturally from love. Third, Jesus is the one who makes it possible for us to rejoice with joy unspeakable. The word "unspeakable" is a compound of *laleō* ("to speak"), *ek* ("out"), and *a*—an alpha privative meaning "no" standing before the rest of the word and negating the usual meaning of the term. Thus the word literally means "not speaking out." It denotes a joy which may be experienced but is of such a nature as to defy adequate verbal expression.

Finally, Peter declares that because of our relationship with Jesus, we have been filled with glory. There is yet to be more glory, but already the disciple is in possession of an inner grandeur that will later be outwardly manifested. The perfect participle is utilized here indicating that his filling with glory happened in the past and that the results continue indefinitely into the future.

Verse 9. The translation "perpetually receiving" is an improved rendering of the present participle. Present tense points to linear or continuing action. From the initiation of salvation, man keeps on receiving the fulfillment of his faith, the salvation of his soul. The word "fulfillment" ("end," KJV) is *telos*. It does mean "end" but is not limited to the idea of extremity. "Just consummation" or "resulting fulfillment" does greater justice to the word. A lengthy period of time may be involved in the *telos*. Such is certainly the case here.

"Soul" is the word *psuchē*. This word is concerned with the life principle as such. It does not mean the earthly body but the essential part of man which exists eternally either in heaven or in hell. It is that part of man which is immediately changeable from fleshly orientation to spiritual orientation. This reference to the salvation of the soul is another evidence that man is actually bipartite. He is body and soul. He has a material nature and a spiritual nature. The latter is called the soul.

The Mystery of Salvation (1:10-12)

10—Of which salvation the prophets have inquired and searched diligently, who prophesied of the grace that should come unto you:

11—Searching what, or what manner of time the Spirit of Christ which was in them did signify, when it testified beforehand the sufferings of Christ, and the glory that should follow.

12—Unto whom it was revealed, that not unto themselves, but unto us they did minister the things, which are now reported unto you by them that have preached the gospel unto you with the Holy Ghost sent down from heaven; which things the angels desire to look into.

Salvation tendered, tried, and triumphant continues to mystify minds limited by worldly thoughts and eyes dimmed by the restriction of human vision alone. Exactly how it is that God can transform a man on the basis of the cross and the instrumentality of the Holy Spirit is a mystery. Enough was known of God for the prophets to be aware of an exciting future in God's plan for man. A cursory reading of the Old Testament will show a consistent interest in the Lord's promised salvation. Some prophets give evidence of having understood more than others concerning the nature of redemption, but all were limited to partial knowledge. Therefore, the mystery of salvation became the subject of extensive prophetic inquiry.

Verses 10-11. The words "that should come" are added for clarity but do not actually appear in the Greek text. The salvation which has thus far been the subject of the discussion is described in terms of grace directed toward the readers of the epistle. This grace had been the *leitmotif* of prophetic pronouncements. In addition, Peter says that the same prophets sought out and searched thoroughly the prophecies, keeping up a continual investigation of the information available about God's grace.

The words "sought out" and "searched thoroughly" are Greek verbs in the aorist tense (viewing the action as a whole) and must be understood in connection with the present participle "continually investigating." The present participle would indicate that incessant investigation was carried on by the prophets. The aorist tenses tell us of the fervency and determined effort which accompanied that search.

Some commentators have conjectured strongly that the prophets under consideration were New Testament prophets rather than the prophets of Israel. While the point yields no certain identification, the use of the tenses favors the view that Israel's prophets are intended. The argument that the prophets had no Bible as such to search is without consequence since even prior to Moses' recording of the Torah, God was making Himself and His will known. The linguistic argument concerning the lack of the article before the word "prophets" is at best inconclusive.

What was it which the prophets investigated? Like the excited post-resurrection disciples who were interested in the time of the restoration of the kingdom to Israel, they were interested in the question "When?" They wished to ascertain, if possible, the time or the kind of time for the fulfillment of those things which the Spirit of Christ was making evident to them. If it were not possible to know exactly when the act of redemption was to be accomplished, then they at least wanted to know what kind of time it would be. That is a peculiar expression. But the word used for time is *kairos* rather than *kronos*. The difference between the two words has already been suggested. *Kairos* time may refer to a chosen time or to a period of time within the usual counting of the years. That for which they evidently sought was the relation of this redemptive event to the coming of the Kingdom of God and His perfect rule on this earth.

We note in verse 11 a clear statement which acquaints us with Peter's view of the inspiration of Scripture. God cannot make mistakes. Peter declares that what these prophets of the Old Testament said concerning the coming expression of grace was being made evident to them by the spirit of Christ. It was not a passing figment of their own over-zealous religious imaginations.

The words "make evident" are the translation of *dēlaō* which may mean "to impart," "to make evident, plain, or clear." What the prophets had to say did not represent their own theological formulation of a few vague general principles loosely impressed upon their minds by some mysterious force. Nor is this a "mechanical dictation" theory of inspiration. It is simply Peter's statement that the Holy Spirit operated in the minds and hearts of the prophets in such a definite way that the truths of God became crystal clear. The writers were kept from error by the clarity of the revelation. Peter obviously trusts their word to be God's revelation. The verb *dēlaō* is used here in the imperfect tense, a tense indicating continuing action in past time. The activity of the Spirit in revelation was not momentary but extended and diverse. Hebrews 1:1 tells of God's speaking at different times and in various ways through the prophets (plural).

Specifically, the Holy Spirit bore witness beforehand to the certainty of Christ's sufferings and the glory which would follow. Isaiah doubtless had an unusual grasp of what kind of Messiah the Suffering Servant would be. Jeremiah had a vision of the resulting glory which would come to the redeemed when he described the coming of spiritual heart transplants. And who could question the glory of Daniel's vision of the Ancient of Days? These are cases of specific information imparted to the minds of God's prophets by the Holy Spirit.

Note that there were two emphatic features of Old Testament prophecy. One facet of prophecy focused on the incarnation and atonement of Jesus. The other featured the glory which would eventually be Christ's at His return and the inauguration of the millennial kingdom. Sometimes both events were a part of the same prophecy. For example, Isaiah 61:1-12 is a declaration of what Christ would accomplish in the atonement and in judgment. Isaiah saw it all in one package. But when Jesus reads the passage in His synagogue sermon in Nazareth (Luke 4:16-21), He omits the last phrase, "and the day of the vengeance of our God," so that He can accurately conclude that the Scripture is fulfilled in their ears that very day. The second phase of that messianic vision awaits the return of Christ in the future.

Verse 12. If the efforts of the prophets failed to uncover the hour of Christ's passion, they did at least learn that their prophecies would be read by a later generation which would see in the events of the life of Jesus the execution of prophetically foretold events. Their work was more than a preaching ministry; as instruments for revelation they actually were ministering to succeeding generations. In fact, their witness was the same as that of the evangels who had recently and successfully proclaimed the gospel to the people living in Asia Minor. The only difference was that the prophets stood on the other side of the cross. Together their witness provided a powerful cumulative effect. The word translated "preached the gospel" is *euangelizomai*. It derives from *eu* ("well" or "good") and *angellō* ("to bring a message"). Thus it means to bring a good message—namely, that of forgiveness of sins and regeneration due to Christ's atonement.

Another significant feature of witness is emphasized by Peter in adding the witness of the Holy Spirit to that of the proclaimers of the good news. Indeed, it is the Holy Spirit alone who causes conviction concerning sin and accomplishes regeneration. His work is essential. However gifted the evangelist, regardless of his sharpened skills and able rhetoric, the battle is lost without the work of the Holy Spirit.

Peter's discussion of the magnitude of our salvation is climaxed by a reminder to the readers that theirs is a fortunate position as the redeemed of the Lord. Even the angelic hosts desire ardently to look into the mystery of redemption. The word "desire" is from *epithumeō*, which is often translated in the King James Version as "lust." The context, however, determines the moral tone of the word. Here it is a wholesome desire which the angels exercise.

"To look" is the translation of *parakuptō* which derives from *para* ("beside") and *kuptō* ("to stoop"). The idea is that of kneeling down in order to examine something carefully. It is the most assiduous scrutiny which the angels desire to expend upon the subject of salvation.

How remarkable is the grace of God that allows us not only merely to examine such salvation but also to experience it!

A Gift with Strings Attached

1. The Profit of the Gift (1:13-17)
2. The Purchase of the Gift (1:18-20)
3. The Purpose of the Gift (1:21-23)
4. The Permanence of the Gift (1:24-25)

Author's Translation (1:13-25)

13—Therefore, while girding up the loins of your understanding, being sober, hope completely upon the grace being brought to you by the revelation of Jesus Christ.

14—As obedient children, not being conformed to the former desires [which were maintained] in your ignorance,

15—But according to the Holy One who called you, you become holy also in all deportment,

16—As it has been written, you shall be holy because I am holy.

17—And since you call upon the Father as one who is judging impartially with reference to the works of each man, conduct yourselves in fear [during] the time of your pilgrimage.

18—Knowing that you were not redeemed out of your unprofitable way of life handed down from your fathers with corruptible things, silver or gold,

19—But by the precious blood of Christ as of a lamb blameless and spotless,

20—Having been foreknown from the foundation of the world, but having been made manifest in the last times because of you,

21—Who through Him trust in God, the one who raised him out of the dead and gave glory to him, so that your faith and hope are in God.

22—Having purified your souls in obedience of the truth unto a sincere love for the brethren, fervently love one another from the heart,

23—Having been born again not out of corruptible seed but incorruptible, through the living and abiding word of God;

24—For all flesh [is] as grass

And all its glory [is] as the flower of the field.

The grass withers

And the flower falls off,

25—But the word of the Lord remains forever. And this is the word which was preached unto you.

The Profit of the Gift (1:13-17)

13—Wherefore gird up the loins of your mind, be sober, and hope to the end for the grace that is to be brought unto you at the revelation of Jesus Christ;

14—As obedient children, not fashioning yourselves according to the former lusts in your ignorance.

15—But as he which hath called you is holy, so be ye holy in all manner of conversation:

16—Because it is written, Be ye holy; for I am holy.

17—And if ye call on the Father, who without respect of persons judgeth according to every man's work, pass the time of your sojourning here in fear:

The introductory portion of First Peter served to remind the Christians of Asia Minor of the immeasurable gift of salvation which God had provided. However, an irresponsible receiver of gifts will not long glory in the gift. God's gift of salvation comes through free grace. Once a man decides to accept the gift, he must assent to the responsibilities that come with heirship. Jesus is not just Savior but also Lord! The remainder of chapter 1 is dedicated to this theme.

Verse 13. The expression "gird up your loins," is a meaningful phrase of Oriental origin which translated into Occidental terminology might be rendered "roll up your sleeves." However, metaphors even more than individual words suffer in translation. Consequently, a look at the phrase in its Eastern context will be helpful.

Long, flowing robes—still a familiar sight in some Middle

Eastern countries—were the customary garb of the people. If it became necessary to expend a large amount of energy in some strenuous activity, the robe would be grasped from the bottom at the back seam, drawn between the legs, and tucked into a large belt worn around the mid-section. This process was called "girding up the loins."

More specifically, in the text this is a metaphor urging strict vigilance in regard to the mind and insight. This is in keeping with the sage of the Old Testament who said, "For as he thinketh in his heart, so is he" (Prov. 23:7), or again, "Keep thy heart with all diligence, for out of it are the issues of life" (Prov. 4:23).

The word translated "understanding" is *dianoia* from *dia* ("through") and *nous* ("mind"). *Nous* is a noun derived from the verb "think," giving this word the sense of "to think through." Actually the word may mean moral attitude, intellectual understanding, or resolve as a function of the will. This verse challenges the dichotomy that has been maintained between intellectual prowess and spiritual power. The two are not diametrically opposed but complementary. The adequate servant of Christ must be a sharpened tool wielded by a powerful Spirit. We are to sharpen ourselves and make a sacrificial present of ourselves to the Lord for a filling of His power and for His use.

While they were sharpening their spiritual understandings, Peter instructed Christians to maintain sobriety. The word "sober" has a double sense in Greek. Literally, according to Otto Bauernfeind, the word means not only freedom from intoxication with wine, but also freedom from all effect of wine.[1] This is unquestionably assumed to be the foundational meaning in this context. The Christian's insistence upon total abstinence is perhaps more important today than ever before. The association of alcohol with death, injury, sickness, and despair is even more real than apparent. Long ago Solomon

---

[1]Kittel, *Theological Dictionary,* vol. IV, p. 936.

cautioned, "Wine is a mocker, strong drink is raging, and whosoever is deceived thereby is not wise" (Prov. 20:1).

But this mandate is also an injunction urging spiritual sobriety. A characteristic of our day is a society constantly in travail, giving birth to new opinions and systems. The word "new" is not inherently evil, but neither is it fundamentally good. Which of us can ever forget the wonderful "new" drug thalidomide, which cursed the lives of so many innocent infants? Or what of the exciting "new" discovery which made atomic fission possible and thereby resulted in mammoth destruction of life? The rise of opinions and systems which propagate ideas and practices in disharmony with God's word has an intoxicating nature.

The universities and graduate schools of America were supposed to be casteless societies in which reputable scholars could pursue freely the conquest of truth and knowledge. Instead, they have often become asylums for the harboring of inmates with inflated egos and minds engulfed with some "new" idea which has little reality outside the classroom. Instead of belching forth discovered truth, too often these institutions have merely dribbled forth the lukewarm liquid of theory which God cannot tolerate and by which man cannot live. Society becomes intoxicated with such pseudo-intellectualism and in this inebriated form is impervious to the demands of the gospel.

Recently I was bearing witness about Christ in the New Orleans French Quarter when two men came by in succession—one quite drunk. The first, when asked if he knew Christ, replied, "I am Jesus." He was drunk with wine. The second replied that he believed in God; but as far as Jesus the Son was concerned, he thought of Him only as Satan's brother. He was physically sober, but the propagation of error left him as helplessly intoxicated as the first. Spiritual sobriety is critical for the Christian. The word is actually a present participle, indicating the necessity of continual sobriety. Christians sometimes become unbalanced, exhibiting unbridled enthusiasm for aspects of the faith which are not central issues. This exhortation to sobriety is a caution to Christians to maintain a Spirit-controlled mind.

A Christian who has maintained sobriety and coordinated his understanding around spiritual matters ought also to be hoping completely in the grace of God which will be his at Christ's coming. The King James Version translates "hope to the end." The word "end," however, is the Greek adverb *teleiōs*, which means "perfectly" or "completely." The totality of the Christian's hope (see meaning of "hope" in 1:3) is in the coming deliverance which will be his at the second advent of Christ. Other hopes may be cherished, but these are singularly destined to disappoint. Only the promised return of the Lord is a reliable hope.

Several words are employed by the New Testament authors to speak of the return of Christ. With the exception of Hebrews 9:28, which speaks of Christ as appearing a second time, the terminology "second coming" is not found. *Erchomai*, which is a general word for "coming," is sometimes used (see Matt. 25:27). *Parousia* is a compound word meaning "to be alongside" or "present." It is used of the return of Christ repeatedly (see Matt. 24:3; 1 Cor. 15:23; *et. al.*). *Epiphaneia* denotes "appearance" and seems generally to emphasize the rather spectacular nature of Christ's return (2 Thess. 2:8; Titus 2:13). Finally, *apokalupsis*, usually rendered "revelation" connotes the unveiling of something that was previously known, at best, only in part. This is the word used in the text here. Christ has been revealed in His incarnation. This revelation was shrouded in the veil of His humanity. The next revelation of Jesus will be a revelation of His glory. Just as the incarnation and atonement were acts of God's grace, so the return of Christ will be grace brought to humanity.

Verse 14. The Christian's conduct in light of God's gracious gift is to be that of an obedient child. Obedient is the translation of *hupakoē*, which is a compound word deriving from *hupo* (under) and *akouō* (to hear). Thus one who is obedient or submissive is one who hears the Master's voice from an admittedly inferior position. The essence of the Christian life is depicted by this word. Any Christian experience must begin by hearing the revelation of God concerning man's disease and God's remedy. Then the act of subordination to Christ, involving repentance and faith, must follow. The order of the words in Greek (children of submissiveness) indicates that the attitude of obedience should be a characteristic of God's children.

On the other hand, the child of God will break all conformity to his former way of life. The phrase "not being conformed" is of special interest. The word is *suschēmatizomenoi* for *sun* ("with" or "together with") and *schema* ("form," "figure," "fashion"). Our word scheme comes from this latter word and carries something of the same meaning. The phrase may be translated "not being fashioned together" with the former desires. Selwyn agrees with Lightfoot that the word *schema* denotes something changeable, fleeting, and unstable.[2] Former desires are to be abandoned because they are temporary and because they are not characteristic of submissive children. In addition, these former desires were held in ignorance. "Ignorance" literally means "no knowledge." Hence the manner of life for a man without Christ is characterized by lack of knowledge.

Verses 15-16. The believer is to occupy a position of holiness based on the holiness of God. The King James Version speaks of holiness in regard to "conversation." However, "deportment" is a broader term including both what one says and what one does. This translation satisfies more completely the idea of the Greek word. *Anastrophē* is the word in question. It is a compound of *ana* ("again" or "up") and *strephō* ("to turn" or "to change"). Christian conduct is marked by a turning or a change which takes one in an upward direction.

This mandate to holiness is based upon a citation of Leviti-

---

[2]Edward G. Selwyn, *The First Epistle of Saint Peter,* p. 141.

cus 11:44, "ye shall be holy; for I am holy." Peter employs the same formula in introducing this Old Testament quotation which he had heard so often on the lips of Jesus. "It is written" is more accurately translated, "it stands written." The Greek verb *gegraptai* is a perfect tense, which in the language of the New Testament refers to a past event the results of which continue indefinitely into the future. Therefore, Peter concludes that what was written by Moses in Leviticus 11:44 remains unchangeably the word of God.

The concept of holiness is too often understood in terms of moral rectitude. The actual significance of the word *hagios* is "separation." The same general definition is applicable to the Hebrew word *qadosh*, also translated "holy."[3] In fact, the whole idea of "holiness" may be observed most profoundly in the distinction attached to the Holy of Holies in the tabernacle or the temple of Solomon. So "set apart" was that place that only the High Priest could enter. And he could do so only on the Day of Atonement and then only with sacrificial blood in hand.

Or again Isaiah repeatedly emphasizes the idea of God's holiness. In Isaiah 6:3 the seraphim shout antiphonally to one another of the thrice holy God. As if anticipating the day when critical scholars would allege dual or even triple authorship of his book, Isaiah in a sense autographed both halves of the work with the relatively unique identification of God as the *Qadosh Israel*, the "Holy One of Israel." Used only five times in the entire Old Testament outside of Isaiah, that prophet used it twenty-nine times, twelve in the first thirty-nine chapters and seventeen times in the remaining half, which is often called deutero-Isaiah.

Ethical and moral purity are certainly involved in holiness. But these are qualities which sparkle as a result of a natural, or should one say, a supernatural difference. God is distinct from all of His creation. God's holiness is the attribute which

---

[3]Kittel, *Theological Dictionary*, vol. I., pp. 88-115.

renders pantheism or the more modern panentheism (the idea that God is somehow in everything) impossible. The command to be holy is therefore a mandate to be categorically distinct from the rest of creation and to be set apart from common use. Holiness begins in the new birth and should progress to moral and ethical purity of life, thus distinguishing God's children from the children of the devil.

Tragically, the loss of a sense of holiness is manifested in Christianity of this era in the absence of church discipline. Even the thought of church discipline is a harrowing experience for most churchmen. Our age has prostituted the virtue of tolerance and recast it as an indiscriminant woman of the night to whom all things are acceptable! What is lost in pulpit and pew is a sense of the holiness of God and the consequent mandate of the Lord for His people to be holy also.

Verse 17. The believer should also maintain an attitude of reverence toward the Father. The King James Version translates the passage as if there were some question about the readers calling on God as Father. However, the Greek particle *ei* may also be translated "since," especially according to Thayer's Lexicon, "When a conclusion is drawn from something that is quite certain."[4] The conclusion being drawn is that men should conduct themselves in fear, and it is certain that the Asian Christians called God "Father." Therefore, because they call Him "Father" and since they recognize that He judges impartially with reference to the works of each man, fear is in order.

The word which we have translated "impartially" is a vivid word in the Greek New Testament. It is the adverb *aprosōpolēmptōs* which is composed of four distinct words. *A* is the alpha privative which negates the rest of the word. The next word *prosōpon* is really two words, *pros* (toward) and *ops* (face). Finally *lambanō* is the verb which means "to receive."

Putting all this together minus the alpha negative, the word

---

[4]Joseph Henry Thayer, *A Greek-English Lexicon of the New Testament*, p. 169.

means "to receive one face to face," or perhaps "to receive one on the limited basis of a facial judgment." Add the negative particle, and it is understood that the heavenly Father does not accept a shallow facial judgment, looking only at the way things outwardly appear. In Mark 7 Jesus spoke of the Pharisees as knowing God verbally while their hearts were far away. But He whose eyes are like a flame of fire sees beyond the apparent and judges on the basis of the real.

The imperative states that the disciple is to conduct himself in fear. Psalm 111:10 noted in a similar vein that "the fear of the Lord is the beginning of wisdom." What do such expressions mean? The word used is *phobeō*. It is a word which has both bad connotations (see 1 John 4:18) and good meanings (as here and as in Acts 9:31). The context will determine whether or not *phobeō* is wholesome. When it is the fear of the Lord, it is, of course, good. The word does not imply a fearful, quaking reticence which would impair fellowship with or inhibit approach to God. On the contrary, we are invited to approach God boldly. But in the language of the New Testament, terms such as boldness and fear are not mutually exclusive. Neither do they constitute an insoluble paradox.

Our understanding of what it means to fear God will be enhanced by a glance at two of the psalms in which the Hebrew word *yirah* (a close equivalent to *phobeō*) is used. In Psalm 34:11ff., David is teaching his children the fear of the Lord. He lists a number of actions, such as departing from evil or seeking peace, as examples of a life of reverence for God. But in verse 16, he declares that God will cut off the remembrance of evil men. In Psalm 2:11 the author exhorts his readers to "serve the Lord with fear, and rejoice with trembling." In other words, legitimate fear of God results from a knowledge of Him. Because we are aware of His indignation against evil and His smile toward the good, we serve Him joyfully and come boldly to Him for His aid.

The time for fearing God is said to be during the time of our pilgrimage. A reference to pilgrims appeared in verse 1, but the word used here is *paroikia,* a different word. The word in verse 1 seems to emphasize the transitory nature of the sojourner's stay, whereas this word refers to the Christian's legal status as a non-citizen.[5] Literally the word means "to dwell beside." The English word "parish" is derived from this word. Whatever the distinctions, the idea of temporality is paramount. Our stay on planet earth should be in deep reverence to God because we dwell here for only a short time.

The Purchase of the Gift (1:18-20)

18—Forasmuch as ye know that ye were not redeemed with corruptible things, as silver and gold, from your vain conversation received by tradition from your fathers;

19—But with the precious blood of Christ, as of a lamb without blemish and without spot:

20—Who verily was foreordained before the foundation of the world, but was manifest in these last times for you.

Verse 18. Reverence (v. 17) is urged upon the readers because of the cost of redemption. There is first a statement repudiating the use of material values in the purchase of salvation. Then a positive statement of the costliness of salvation is framed in verse 19. Negatively, the kind of redemption needed by man (victory over death) cannot be achieved through the expenditure of corruptible currency. All the silver and gold is the property of God, but its relative value as compared to one man is negligible. So redemption is basically out of the sphere of materialistic values altogether. The reason is evident when man's predicament is properly viewed.

Man needs deliverance from unprofitableness. The word is *mataia,* and it denotes the world of appearance as distinct from that of real being. Superior technology, vaunted space programs, devastating arsenals, philosophical skills, and

---

[5]Selwyn, *First Epistle of Saint Peter,* p. 118.

medical successes elevate man. He appears to be in the driver's seat—serene and domineering. In reality the steering column is disconnected and the foot pedals useless. A crash is certain, and man is inwardly frightened. From this unprofitable and fruitless condition which was handed down from his ancestors, man needs to be rescued.

Out of the midst of a life of this sort, the believer has been redeemed. This redemption was thoroughly accomplished in the atoning death of Jesus. The word "redeem" is the translation of the verb *lutroō*. Etymologically, it derives from *luo* meaning "to loose." The idea of loosing the penitent from the grasp of sin is an important emphasis of the word. But the *lutroō* word group is commonly used in secular Greek and always involves a purchase. The *tron* suffix which appears in the noun denotes basically the means by which an action is performed. In the Greek of the New Testament era, *tron* often had reference to payment.[6] Accordingly, the sense of *lutroō* is payment or ransom to secure escape from the clutches of sin. It is a word not infrequently associated with the slave market.

Thus Peter declares that man's lot is irrevocably cast with his ancestors through sin. He is both helpless and hopeless—a slave to his own passions and desires. Redemption is effected by Christ, and the receiving of that salvation constitutes man's only hope for freedom. But observe the redemptive price!

Verse 19. The price paid was the precious blood of Christ. The word "precious" means "highly esteemed," "valuable." It is so because Christ is the Lamb who is blameless and spotless. Old Testament sacrificial animals were to be the best in the flock. The language of verse 19 is clearly that same sacrificial language with respect to the only adequate lamb—Jesus Christ. Jesus is blameless. He has done nothing to incur blame. He is spotless and untainted by sin or impurity of any variety. Therefore, His sacrifice was precious indeed.

---

[6]Leon Morris, *The Apostolic Preaching of the Cross*, p. 9.

The language of redemption is unpleasant *to some*. One theologian has written recently, "It is quite possible to affirm and clarify the importance of the cross without speaking of it as necessary."[7] The same author says:

> Men today do not ordinarily hold this view of God as simply willing right and wrong, and so they cannot believe that vicarious punishment is either meaningful or moral. No illustration can be given, so far as I can tell, which makes vicarious punishment morally credible to men today. . . . It always seems morally outrageous that any judge would require a substitute. However noble the substitute's act might be, the judge's act seems despicable.[8]

How one can champion such a position in light of Peter's clear statement that we are redeemed by the precious blood of Christ is a mystery. Still less can the view that the atonement was not "necessary" or "substitutionary" be justified in the light of Romans 3:25-26 which declares that Christ's blood was a propitiatory sacrifice which declared God's righteousness by making it possible for God to justify believers and still be absolutely just in so doing.

The idea of redemption and a sacrificial price for man's freedom is distasteful *to many* whose humanism has not been sufficiently shaken by the ravages of sin. But this is just the point. Through the sufferings of Jesus, God demonstrated the despicableness and horror of sin. In light of the shameful cross (the work of religious and political leaders to remove the offensive Christ), no one can doubt the ignominy of sin. Further, God has taken upon himself the punishment for sin in the death of Jesus on the cross. The language of the New Testament, especially this passage, emphasizes the ransom factor in the redemption of man.

The blood of Christ is also declared to be without blemish

---

[7]Fisher Humphreys, *The Death of Christ*, p. 55.
[8]*Ibid.*, p. 61.

or spot. Literally the words may be rendered "blameless" and "pure." This is Peter's further method of affirming the rationale for the atonement. The blood of Christ redeems because it represents a blameless and pure life given as a substitute for sinners who, according to the law, must die (see Ezek. 18:4). The soul that sins must die, but Jesus, the Sinless One, shed His blood in behalf of sinners. This is nothing less than vicarious, substitutionary death, satisfying or propitiating the just demands of a righteous and holy God.

Verse 20. Finally, Peter broaches the question as to the time of redemption. Men have always been redeemed as a result of the same basic principle—namely, God's grace and man's faith to receive that grace. This is possible because the spotless Lamb and His atoning sacrifice were foreknown by God through the ageless eons of time prior to the founding of earth or the creation of man. But, while the men of the Old Testament looked for promised redemption, they could not begin to assimilate salvation's magnitude as could men who have experienced God's revelation of Himself in Christ. In these last times, Christ was made manifest for the benefit of the readers and even for the whole world.

The Purpose of the Gift (1:21-23)

21—Who by him do believe in God, that raised him up from the dead, and gave him glory; that your faith and hope might be in God.
22—Seeing ye have purified your souls in obeying the truth through the Spirit unto unfeigned love of the brethren, see that ye love one another with a pure heart fervently:
23—Being born again, not of corruptible seed, but of incorruptible, by the word of God, which liveth and abideth for ever.

Verse 21. The marvelous gift which God has given enables men to trust in God. The mediatorial significance of Christ is nowhere more clearly established. One may claim faith in God and still be unacceptable to the omniscient Judge. True faith in God always acknowledges God's revelation of Himself in Christ and relies upon the atonement made by Jesus to be the remedy for sin. A commitment of life is made to Christ, and saving faith is present.

The verse further declares that our faith and hope are in God as a result of the resurrection of Christ and the glory given to Him by the Father. The logic is incontrovertible. If you wish to persuade a man that a certain medication will cure his cancerous lungs which formerly he had been led to conclude are incurable, show him a man who is healthy as a result of the proposed solution. If we desire to speak to dying men about the certainty of death, and still hold a hope before them, then we must know of one who *was* dead and *is* alive! Thus we point to Jesus and assert that in Christ death was given an irreparable blow. The sting is removed, and the grave has no victory. By trusting in a living Christ, man places his faith and hope in God. Faith directs his life in the present age, while his hope frees him to anticipate eternity without fear.

Verse 22. "Having purified" is a perfect participle in Greek. It points to a definite past action, the results of which are still abiding with us. God's imputed righteousness is an instantaneous miracle which purifies the impure, vivifies the lifeless, and justifies the spiritual criminal. The results of this miracle never depart from the believer and ultimately climax in the heavenly state. The words "having purified" could appear to place man in the position of purifying himself. However, the verse teaches us the opposite. It is in obedience to truth that man's soul is purified. What truth is intended? The one about which the writer has been speaking in verses 18 through 20—the atoning blood of Jesus Christ. If man responds in faith to this gracious gift, then he has taken the only step toward God and resulting purity which he can take. Even this step is a result of the conviction brought by the Spirit of God.

Sincere love of the brethren is the hallmark of discipleship according to Jesus (John 13:35). It is also one of the fruits of a purified soul. The word sincere is *anupokritos,* which is the word usually translated as "hypocrite" prefixed by the alpha negative. Thus it signifies a love void of hypocrisy. The word "hypocrite" designated one who donned a mask and played a role in a drama. A hypocrite is, therefore, one who is just acting behind the facade of a mask. He is a cheap imitation of the real.

Love for our brethren in the faith is to be genuine. The Epistle of James describes hypocritical love as that which says to the hungry man, "be filled" and to the naked, "be clothed." Notwithstanding, nothing is done to alleviate such suffering. Love for the brethren which is genuine will do what it can to meet the need. Thus, Peter emphasizes the matter of love again, this time saying, "fervently love one another from the heart." "Fervently" is the translation of *ektenōs* which derives from a word meaning "to stretch out." Stretching out takes effort and causes a tension. Hence our translation "fervent." In Acts 12:5 the word is used to describe the prayers of the Jerusalem church in behalf of imprisoned Simon Peter. It is said that the church prayed "without ceasing" *(ektenōs).* Stretching ourselves out in love is a vital aspect of Christianity which must be deed as well as word.

The point of origin for this love is emphasized in the Greek Testament by the position of the words "out of the heart." In Scripture, the heart is used to denote the most basic convictions and attitudes of a man upon which foundation all other aspects of life are constructed. Thus, Jesus says it is "from within, out of the heart," that evil thoughts proceed (see Mark 7:21). Again, wherever your treasure is "there will your heart be also" (Matt. 6:21). Similarly, it is with all his heart (see Matt. 22:37) that man is to love the Lord. The admonition of Peter is a challenge to make love for one another a basic foundation for our service to Christ and to others.

A word must also be said about what it means to love. The theology of Love has become the champion of the day. Love is such a noble word and nothing can be said against it. Joseph

Fletcher has popularized the "love ethic" in his *Situation Ethics*. He says, "Only the commandment to love is categorically good."[9] John A. T. Robinson says the same from a negative approach.

> For nothing can of itself be labelled as 'wrong.' One cannot, for instance, start from the proposition 'sex relations before marriage' or 'divorce,' are wrong and sinful in themselves. They may be in 99 cases or even 100 cases out of a hundred, but they are not intrinsically so, for the only intrinsic evil is lack of love.[10]

Let it be emphatically noted that the love which Peter, and indeed all of the Bible, urges is not a love which is void of context. It is not love without the law or regardless of the law but love through the law. God's laws are not relative. There are constants in God's plan and to flout them is to rebel against the Creator and fail to love Him as we ought. Fletcher and Robinson both suffer from the effects of a humanistic, man-centered love which does not take seriously the first of the dual command regarding love. Peter is saying that men ought to love one another in imitation of the way God loves man.

Verse 23. God's gift of Himself in Jesus enables us to trust in God, to have purified lives, to love the brethren, and finally, to have a transformed, incorruptible existence. "Having been born again" is a one-word perfect participle in the Greek. The perfect tense points to the former event, the consequences of which continue. The word comes from *ana* ("again") and *gennaō* ("to begat" or "to be born"). Christianity is always in danger of allowing external functions or even processes to stand in the place of a new beginning. But the radical and instantaneous nature of regeneration or the initiation of salvation is described by the New Testament as "being born again."

---

[9]Joseph Fletcher, *Situation Ethics: The New Morality,* p. 26.

[10]John A. T. Robinson, *Honest to God,* p. 118.

Anything less than a dramatic encounter with Christ resulting in regeneration and new life is insufficient to secure salvation.

The seed of this new life does not have within it the inherent corruption of the seed which begat man in his physical existence. All the staggering successes of medical science have failed to produce anything like an indestructible man. Our physical body is subject to decay, and that process continues until death overtakes life.

As a boy, I enjoyed western movies and television shows. Toward the climax of each movie, the last and most vicious of the villains would leap on his horse and race out of town. The hero would follow on his swift steed. Across the countryside they would race, with the hero gradually gaining on the culprit. At last the guy with the white hat would draw alongside the guy with the black hat. In a spectacular exhibition of acrobatics, the hero would fly through the air; and both men would tumble to the ground and down a hill, marvellously, without breaking a bone or even losing their hats.

In more mature years I have often seen life as racing across the stage, fleeing the evergaining pale horse of death. But the chances of life's winning the race are less than that of the villain in the western. Death always catches life. So Peter declares God's answer to this. The effects of the first birth may be successfully apprehended by death, but it is an empty victory if the second birth is present. Sin and death, having gained the victory over the first birth, find themselves grappling with a foe which spells defeat for death because the seed of the new birth is incorruptible. It is incorruptible because it is made available through "the living and abiding word of God."

Does the phrase "Word of God" refer to the Bible or to Christ? In John's gospel and in the Apocalypse, the phrase unquestionably refers to Christ. However, the understanding of Christ as the divine communication (the Word) of God to man is deeply embedded in the New Testament. The Bible is the primary witness to Christ the Word. Its words will make us "wise unto salvation" (2 Tim. 3:15). Furthermore, Peter's reference to Isaiah 40:8 doubtless refers primarily to the written or prophetic word of God. But the Bible is neither the atonement for our sins nor the regenerative force in the new birth. Christ accomplished that atonement and is the cause of the new birth. So "Word," while including the Bible, here refers to Christ. He is the living Word, and it is the fact and permanence of His life which guarantees our own. He is the abiding Word, and the promise of His presence is the foundation upon which the believer may rest securely.

The Permanence of the Gift (1:24-25)

24—For all flesh is as grass, and all the glory of man as the flower or grass. The grass withereth, and the flower thereof falleth away:

25—But the word of the Lord endureth for ever. And this is the word which by the gospel is preached unto you.

Verse 24. The transient quality of life is further emphasized in verse 24 and contrasted with the eternality of Christ the Word. The renewed emphasis upon life in Christ alerts the reader to the apostle's desire to pit the immutable virtues of Christ against the temporary and limited sphere of physical life. The reader is reminded that this epistle is concerned with the suffering of the righteous. Peter's point is like that of Paul's: "I reckon that the sufferings of this present time are not worthy to be compared with the glory which shall be revealed in us" (Rom. 8:18). The suffering can be tolerated because the believer is looking for another life and another city.

Peter compares life in the flesh to grass and the glories of life to the flowers of the field. The analogies are especially useful. Beautiful green grass sparkles with life. Each flower has a glory of its own. Some have such variegated schemes as to astound us with their natural beauty. Both grass and flowers have one other thing in common. They do not last. The azaleas of southern Louisiana are a startling sight for a few days. But their limited tenure soon expires, and the flower falls off. So it is with life.

The verbs "withered" and "falls off" are both in the aorist tense in Greek, indicating a complete and final action. The word rendered "falls off" is from *ekpiptō* meaning literally "to fall out of." The rose bush continues to live, but the flower withers and falls out of the bush. Life, too, continues until God consummates earthly time, but one by one men, as flowers, fall from the realm of the living.

It should be noted that Peter has quoted Scripture to give further validity to his thesis. Isaiah 40:8 is the passage which he has marshalled to add strength to his argument. It obviously never occurred to Peter to question the inspiration or authority of Scripture. God's written revelation in the Old Testament was definitive.

Verse 25. In contrast to the transient quality of life, the Word of the Lord, Jesus Christ, "goes on abiding into the ages," as the text may be literally translated. A. H. Strong has defined the eternity of God as follows:

> By this we mean that God's nature (a) is without beginning or end; (b) is free from all succession of time; and (c) contains in itself the cause of time.[11]

Peter is affirming that God is transcendent in regard to time and yet immanent in it through His revelation. It is this eternal, abiding Christ who was preached as good news— God revealing Himself in Christ—to the recipients of this letter.

At the close of a service in the little coal mining town of Shime, Japan, on the southern island of Kyushu, an elderly Buddhist man came forward to confess his faith in Christ. His eyes were moist with tears as he said, "I never realized that I could personally know the great God, but I know Him now in Jesus." Peter is saying just that. In Christ the eternal has invaded the temporal!

---

[11]A. H. Strong, *Systematic Theology,* p. 275.

Zion's Patriots and Megapolis

1. Zion's Growing Patriots (2:1-3)
2. Zion's Committed Patriots (2:4-8)
3. Zion's Serving Patriots (2:9-10)

Author's Translation (2:1-10)

1—Therefore laying aside all wickedness and all deceit and hypocrisy, and jealousy and all slander,

2—As newborn babies, have strong affection for the sincere milk of the word in order that you may grow by it into salvation,

3—If you have tasted the graciousness of the Lord.

4—Coming to Him, a living stone, being rejected by men but in the presence of God chosen and precious.

5—And you as living stones are constructing a spiritual house for a holy priesthood to offer up spiritual sacrifices pleasing to God through Jesus Christ.

6—For it is contained in scripture, Behold I place in Zion a choice stone; a precious cornerstone and the one who believes upon Him shall not be ashamed.

7—To you, therefore, who are believing, [He is] the precious one, but to the unbelieving, the stone which the ones who are building rejected, the same has become the head of the corner,

8—and, a stone of stumbling and a rock of destruction [to the ones] who go on stumbling, being disobedient to the word unto which also they were appointed.

9—But you are a chosen race, a kingdom of priests, a holy nation, a people for a possession, in order that you might proclaim the excellencies of the one who called you out of darkness into his wondrous light.

10—Who once [were] not a people but now [are] the people of God; who had not received mercy but now have received mercy.

Zion's Growing Patriots (2:1-3)

1—Wherefore laying aside all malice, and all guile, and hypocrisies, and envies, and all evil speakings,

2—As newborn babes, desire the sincere milk of the word, that ye may grow thereby:

3—If so be ye have tasted that the Lord is gracious.

Regeneration is only the beginning of the Christian life. A man who has become a citizen of Zion through the new birth continues to live in the megapolis, but fundamental alterations ought to begin to occur in his lifestyle. Verse 1 invites him to relinquish the harmful, verse 2 urges him to rally to the helpful, while verse 3 provides the rationale through recognizing the heritage.

Verse 1. Some attitudes and actions simply must be jettisoned in the Christ-life. "Laying aside" is a translation of the participle *apothemenoi* which is a compound word constructed from *tithēmi*, meaning "to place" and the preposition *apo* meaning "from." Five actions and attitudes literally are to be placed away from the life of the believer. The five words, and the principal idea in each word, are graphed below.

KJV	Greek	Fuller Meaning
malice	*kakia*	evil, absence of the good
guile	*dolos*	deceit, fraud, guile
hypocrisies	*hupokrisis*	to pretend, to act out a role
envies	*phthonos*	envy, jealousy
evil speakings	*katalalia*	to criticize, to calumniate

Although all five concepts may generate overt acts, three of the five terms, *kakia*, *dolos*, and *phthonos*, represent atti-

[68]

tudes while *hupokrisis* and *katalalia* are actions that naturally derive from the three attitudes. Grundmann argues that *kakia*, or malice, is the opposite of *agathos*, or good. Hence, it is the absence of good.[1] In Mark 7:21, Jesus says that the heart is the seat of evil *(kakos)*. Paul argues in Romans 13:3-4 that the role of government is primarily to restrain evil *(kakos)*. Putting all this together, *kakia* apparently refers to the absence of good or depravity, which serves as a vacuum in which all manner of sin is spawned.

"Deceit" *(dolos)* is a general departure from truthfulness which eventually comes to fruition in hypocrisies. This latter term literally means "to judge beneath," and has reference to Greek tragedies and comedies in which actors often represented several characters in the same drama by the simple expedients of changing facial masks and disguising the voice. Hence, if you wished to know the real identity of the actor, you must "judge under the mask." The word evolved to mean one who pretended to be something which he was not.

"Envy" *(phthonos)* demonstrates a dissatisfaction and lack of contentment with one's status in life or with one's material possessions. It is the opposite of the contentment enjoined upon believers (1 Tim. 6:8). The frequent upshot of envy is to become critical or even to calumniate or knowingly to misrepresent others. The Greek word *katalalia* covers both since it literally means "to speak down."

Evil in general, together with deceit and envy, are not to be tolerated in the believer's heart. Spiritual pretending and a harsh criitcal spirit must also be eliminated from his life. This is the natural result of the spiritual new birth that has made the Holy Spirit a resident of his life.

Verse 2. Just as there are harmful attitudes and actions to relinquish, so there are positive steps to be taken. Specifically, as a newborn infant seeks sustenance at the breast of the mother, believers are avidly to seek sustenance from the un-

---

[1]Kittel, *Theological Dictionary*, Vol. III, p. 469.

adulterated milk of the word of God. There is surely a play on words here. In verse 1 Peter cautioned about an attitude of deceit *(dolos)* in the heart of believers. In verse 2 the word "sincere" is *adolos* meaning that the word of God, in stark contrast to the proclivities of the human heart, is void of deceit. The term rendered "word" is not the anticipated *logos*, but another form of the word *logikos*, which, as one might suspect, gave us the loan word "logical." The emphasis here is upon the desirability of the mind of God presented in the word of God. The word of God is neither irrational nor arational any more than is the mind of God. Just as the mind of God is sometimes suprarational, so His word may be suprarational since it represents a portion of the mind of God revealed to man.

The expression "desire" is a vivid and poignant word. In Greek, *epipotheō* is a combination of the preposition *epi* (upon) and *potheō*. According to Liddell and Scott, the verb form carries such vigorous ideas as "to long for," "to yearn after," or even "to crave."[2] The prefixed preposition translated "upon" adds double emphasis to an already strong word. Hence the believer is instructed that he is to forsake some attitudes and actions while he develops such a taste for the milk of God's word that he experiences craving upon craving for the word. That kind of desire is the product of genuine love.

The reason for desiring God's word follows. One desires the milk of the word in order that he may grow. The verb "grow" is in the subjunctive mood in Greek, indicating a condition that does not exist and may never exist. In other words, growth in Christ is largely dependent upon a heartfelt desire for the word. In the overwhelming majority of ancient texts and manuscripts the wording of that last phrase is "that ye may grow thereby into salvation." At first glance this might be thought problematic since it seems to suggest the idea that

---

[2]Henry George Liddell and Robert Scott, *A Greek-English Lexicon*, p. 1427.

one may gradually grow into salvation. But 1:23 has already provided Peter's view of salvation as a "birth." In reality, this is another one of those cases like Acts 2:38 and Luke 11:32 where the Greek preposition *eis* (unto) should be rendered "because of." Desiring the milk of the word and growing as a result of that nurture are the consequences of the salvation and not the method of obtaining salvation.

Verse 3. The apostle urges the rejections and positive actions of the first two verses on the basis of the experience of the believer with the Lord. The admonitions of the first two verses are based upon tasting that the Lord is gracious. A vivid metaphor is employed when Peter spoke of "tasting." Although all sense perception is varied, smell and taste are capable of the most excruciating and delightful extremes. Peter, whom on the pages of Scripture we frequently find involved in eating, couches the experience of the believer with God in terms of satisfying taste. Having experienced this good taste, Peter concludes that we will surely desire more.

Zion's Committed Patriots (2:4-8)

4—To whom coming, as unto a living stone, disallowed indeed of men, but chosen of God, and precious,

5—Ye also, as lively stones, are built up a spiritual house, a holy priesthood, to offer up spiritual sacrifices, acceptable to God by Jesus Christ.

6—Wherefore also it is contained in the scripture, Behold, I lay in Zion a chief corner stone, elect, precious: and he that believeth on him shall not be confounded.

7—Unto you therefore which believe he is precious: but unto them which be disobedient, the stone which the builders disallowed, the same is made the head of the corner.

8—And a stone of stumbling, and a rock of offense, even to them which stumble at the word, being disobedient: whereunto also they were appointed.

Zion's patriots are not only growing but also are committed. In verse 4, one may observe the person of the commitment; in verses 5-6, the purpose of the commitment; and in verses 7-8, the pertinence of the commitment. The following passage is especially strategic as an analysis of the tragically misrepresented doctrine of the priesthood of the believer.

Verse 4. Zion's patriots have a commitment to a person who is described as a living stone. Again the metaphor is rich. Stones are never featured as "living." Yet the metaphor suggests strength and life simultaneously. The phrase utilizes the Greek present participle, emphasizing the continuing nature of the life of Christ. Response to the living stone is on three levels. The elect are continually coming (present participle) to the living stone. Most men "disallow" this living stone as useless. But God chooses Him and views Him as precious.

The word "disallow" is a translation of *apodedokimasmenon.* A number of features are intriguing in this word. First, it is a perfect participle. Perfect tense indicates past action with results continuing indefinitely. Hence those who finally reject this living stone involve themselves irremediably in that rejection. Second, the word is from *dokimazō,* which means "to test" or "to examine," and a preposition *apo,* which establishes direction as being "away from." Having examined the living stone some make summary judgment, pushing him away. The phrase is actually borrowed from Psalm 118:22 in the *Septuagint.* The translators of the *Septuagint* had used the word as a rendering of the Hebrew *ma'as,* which means anything from "lightly esteem" to "despise."[3] Both Hebrew and Greek words reflect attitudes toward the living stone ranging from light esteem to hatred. For whichever of those reasons, most men reject the living stone.

But God has chosen the stone which men cast away. The word "chosen" is actually a noun which is usually translated "elect." But Christ, the living stone, is not merely chosen of God, He is precious to God. The anticipated *timios* is intensified by Peter with the preposition *en* making *entimos* as exceedingly precious in and of itself.

---

[3]Francis Brown, S. R. Driver, and Charles A. Briggs, *Hebrew and English Lexicon of the Old Testament,* p. 549.

Verse 5. Four avowals are made concerning those who come to Christ, the living stone. (1) They themselves spring to life as living stones. (2) Corporately they are built into a spiritual house. (3) Within that spiritual citadel they serve individually as a holy priesthood. (4) The function of that priesthood is to offer up spiritual sacrifices acceptable to God through Jesus Christ. Each facet adds critical information about the nature of our faith.

First, life comes from contact with Christ. He is the perpetually living stone chosen of God. Being built around Him is the only way that the life of Christ is transferable to us. However, we do not stand alone. Together with other "living stones," we become a "spiritual house," a metaphor which yields itself nicely to the concept of a believer's church. This is the precise point at which the Swiss and South German Anabaptists such as Conrad Grebel, Felix Manz, Balthasar Hubmaier, and Pilgram Marpeck moved beyond the reformers like Luther, Calvin, and Zwingli and consistently applied the principle of *sola fide*. The Anabaptists saw that a spiritual house or a church could only be constructed out of living stones, that is, men who had experienced regeneration by coming to Christ. Franklin Littell reminds us that the Anabaptists said of Luther and Zwingli that they tore down the old house but built nothing in its place. The Anabaptists considered themselves to be gathering and discipling a true church (*rechte Kirche*).[4]

The function of individual believers within that spiritual house is discussed in terms of a holy priesthood. Thus the doctrine of the priesthood of all believers is placed before the reader. A distorted concept of the priesthood of the believer has become a haven for those who wish to espouse heretical doctrines in the present era. Some argue that their privileged position as believer-priests is jeopardized whenever they are challenged in any way about their beliefs. These aver that the

---

[4]Franklin H. Littell, *The Anabaptist View of the Church* (Boston: Starr King Press, 1958), pp. xvii-2.

priesthood of the believer guarantees them the right to believe just about anything they wish and to interpret the Scriptures in any way which seems expedient.

As I have pointed out elsewhere, the doctrine of the priesthood of believers is a doctrine more concerned with responsibility than with privilege. It is true that the high priest of Israel alone had the privilege of entering the Holy of Holies, but the ominous and awesome nature of that act is evident when one begins to observe the strident limitations placed upon that high priest as to clothing, time of entrance, frequency of entrance, and method of entrance. The greater emphasis is upon the responsibility of that priest in representing the people before God.[5]

The privilege of personal, direct access to God is without doubt a vital aspect of the doctrine. But both verses 5 and 9 say little about the privilege, concentrating instead on the responsibility. Priesthood is not the liberty to interpret the Bible in any way one wishes. Neither is it the liberty to reject any portion of the Bible. The purpose of the priesthood of believers is to offer up spiritual sacrifices which are well pleasing to God. The word translated "acceptable" is *euprosdektos* in the Greek Testament. The *eu* is a prefix meaning "good" or "well." Thus the word literally means "to receive before well" or to present before God well-pleasing sacrifices. What kind of sacrifices are intended?

(1) The believer's body is to be offered to God as a living sacrifice (see Rom. 12:1).

(2) Generous sacrificial offerings of monetary possessions are desirable spiritual sacrifices (see Phil. 4:18).

(3) Compassion for the ignorant and for the lost are imperative spiritual sacrifices (see Heb. 5:1-2).

(4) A spiritual sacrifice of praise is treasured by God (see Heb. 13:15).

---

[5]See my *Shophar Paper*, vol. 2, *Authority and the Priesthood of the Believer*, for more complete discussion. These are available through the Criswell Center for Biblical Studies.

(5) Prayer is a sweet-smelling spiritual sacrifice unto God (see Rev. 8:3).

Nothing is withheld in sacrifice. The life of a sacrificial victim is poured out. By the same token, the doctrine of the priesthood of the believer is involved in total abandonment of oneself to God in all five categories listed above.

Verse 6. Peter now returns to his central thought—Christ, the living stone. Referring to Isaiah 28:16, he begins to exhibit the pertinency of a commitment to Christ. Reasserting the elect and precious nature of Christ, the living stone, the apostle now adds information further demonstrating the relationship between Christ, the living stone, and believers as other living stones. Christ is not just a living stone but also the cornerstone. This metaphor is apparently intended to present Christ as the one who gives both identity and symmetry to the spiritual house which is constituted of the individual believer priests.

Actually verses 6-8 are a combination of three Old Testament passages whose ambit includes Isaiah 28:16, Psalm 118:22, and Isaiah 8:14. The general structure of the passage is as follows:

(1) Christ is the elect, precious cornerstone (see Is. 28:16).

(2) Those who believe in Him shall not be ashamed (see Is. 28:16).

(3) He has been rejected by men but is made by God the head of the corner (see Ps. 118:22).

(4) To some, however, He becomes a stone of stumbling and a rock of offense (see Is. 8:14).

Echoes of these Old Testament passages are found in Romans 9:33, Acts 4:11, Ephesians 2:20, and on the lips of Jesus in Mark 12:10-11, Matthew 21:42, and Luke 20:17. That three gospels recall Jesus' citing the passage with obvious messianic intent establishes the cruciality of the passage. Paul employs the same quote, and Peter uses it in his Acts 4 address as well as in his epistle. It is refreshing to read Selwyn's analysis of the frequent occurrence. Rather than adopting the usual conclusion of critical scholars that Peter borrowed from Paul or the reverse, Selwyn suggests that the Psalm 118 quote and the two quotes from Isaiah were in that order, a part of an early Christian hymn based upon the Savior's own use of the psalm.[6]

The suggestion of the presence of an early hymn in the New Testament text becomes wearisome to conservative scholars who suspect that the motive behind such frequent suggestions is to call into question the full inspiration and authority of portions of the Bible by casting doubt as to whether the real source of a passage is the Holy Spirit. On the other hand, Colossians 3:16 does plainly indicate that the singing of psalms, hymns, and spiritual songs was a recommended method of teaching and admonition in the early church:

> Let the word of Christ dwell in you richly in all wisdom; teaching and admonishing one another in psalms and hymns and spiritual songs, singing with grace in your hearts to the Lord.

That singing was indeed a primary method of theological instruction in the early church is logical in the light of three observations: (1) If those early hymns were composed of excerpts and combination of quotations from the Old Testament, it follows that the use of such hymns would be a part of the pedagogy of the early church. (2) Especially is this so since what one learns musically tends to remain in his mind more permanently than that learned in most other ways. (3) Furthermore, confirmation is lent to such a conclusion by our own experience. From childhood I have known

> Jesus loves me, this I know
> For the Bible tells me so.
> Little ones to Him belong
> They are weak but He is strong.

---

[6]Selwyn, *First Epistle of Saint Peter,* pp. 268-277.

Jesus loves me, He who died
Heaven's gates to open wide.
He will wash away my sin,
Let His little child come in.

While this is not Scripture quotation, consider the theology that it taught me.

(1) Jesus loves me.

(2) I know this because the Bible, which is infallible and inerrant, tells me so.

(3) Those dying before an age of accountability belong to Him.

(4) Men are weak and helpless but He is able.

(5) Christ's death on the cross is that which paves the way for access to God.

(6) Men are sinners and must have that sin cleansed.

(7) Once cleansed, we can enter God's abode.

Before I could read the Bible, those concepts had already found lodging in my mind through the medium of song. Consequently, I do not find objectionable Selwyn's suggestion that the three quotations blended together in this passage actually constituted an early Christian hymn. Inspiration is not affected at all thereby, for the Spirit of God could certainly have moved Peter to use this hymn composed of previously inspired Scripture. Of course, this conclusion is not necessary. Its appeal lies in what it suggests to us of the life of the early church.

Whatever the case may be, two additional features deserve comment. First, even if the three quotations were an early hymn, Peter's appeal is not to the hymnal. "It is contained in Scripture" shows once more the apostle's total confidence in the reliability of God's word. Second, those who believe or trust in Him will not be confounded. The word translated "confounded" is *kataischunthē,* which literally means "shall not be made ashamed." The Hebrew text of Isaiah 18:16 uses *chush,* which is properly rendered "shall not make haste" in the King James Version. The translators of the *Septuagint,* which Peter quotes, translated *chush* with the Greek *kataischunō* "to make ashamed." The translation certainly was accurate since those who believe on Christ will never have to make haste because they are ashamed before Him. This is precisely what John meant when he said in 1 John 2:28, "And now, little children, abide in him; that, when he shall appear, we may have confidence, and not be ashamed before him at his coming."

Verse 7. For those who believe, Christ is precious. Their attitude toward Jesus is precisely the same as God's (v. 6). By contrast, those who are disobedient (*apistousin*—"unbelieving") find themselves necessarily related to Christ in three ways, one of which is mentioned in this verse while two are displayed in verse 8. In other words, one has no choice at all about sustaining some kind of relationship with Christ—he has only a choice about what kind of relationship that will be!

Whereas believers become living stones built into a spiritual building along with Christ the elect cornerstone and are consequently not confounded, unbelievers are ultimately humiliated. The initial humiliation comes when the discovery is made that the very one who has been rejected by them has been chosen by God to the head of the corner. Several matters demand attention. First, note that the builders reject Christ. Here is a classic contrast between the feeble work efforts of man to build his life, his world, even his acceptability with God. His best efforts fail because God must be the building. Second, his efforts fail because he rejects (see exegesis of verse 4) the Savior. He disallows the one element that would bring meaning.

Finally, the unbelieving reject Christ only to find to their shame that God has made Jesus the head of the corner. The unbeliever discovers that he has rejected what God has chosen and hence is ashamed. The affirmation also declares the preeminence of Christ as head of the church.

Verse 8. The unbeliever further discovers that Christ is a stone of stumbling and a rock of offense. "Stumbling" is *proskommatos* which derives from *koptō* (to cut off) and *pros* (toward). The word means "stumbling," and one can see how it came to mean this. Literally it means "to be cut down." "Offense" is *skandalon*, which provides our English word "scandal." The idea of the verse is that the unbeliever eventually finds himself not only ashamed (v. 6), but also cut down and scandalized. Particularly, those who are unbelievers stumble over the word. They do so because of disobedience.

But the word translated "disobedient" here is altogether different from that in the verse above. There it was *apistousin*. This is *pistis* or "faith" with an alpha privative or negative affixed, hence meaning "without faith." But "disobedient" in verse 8 is a pregnant term, *apeithountes*. The verb *peitheō* means "to persuade." Again, the alpha privative means "unpersuaded." Consequently, it is not ignorance or even lack of belief that causes men to be lost. Rather it is a determined predisposition not to be persuaded regardless of the facts. The New Testament uses this term more frequently than any other to describe unbelief so that it will be apparent that men choose their own condemnation.

The final phrase "unto which also they were appointed" is the joy of every full-orbed Calvinistic theologian who argues for double predestination. The account testifies, some suggest, that those who are disobedient were appointed by God for that fate. They were made to be damned in order to exhibit the justice of God. The absurdity of that line of reasoning is at three points.

(1) God surely displays His justice sufficiently in the judgment of Satan and the fallen angels.

(2) To thrust such an interpretation upon these words of Peter does injustice to the fisherman's mental health. In Second Peter 3:9 the same apostle presents God as "not willing that any should perish, but that all should come to repentance." Now there are only three choices. (A) God is talking out of both sides of His mouth, saying then that some are made to be damned and now that He does not want it that

way, and Peter never saw the problem. (B) Peter is suffi- ciently bereft of logic and consistency as to adjust his theol- ogy to meet his whim. (C) The statements are both true but the "whereunto also they were appointed" statement means something other than what some interpreters have imagined. Since only the last option is an evangelical possibility, one is brought to the proper explanation which itself is the third and final reason for rejecting the traditional Calvinistic treatment.

(3) "Appointed" is a translation of *etethēsan*, meaning "to place" or "to set." There is nothing necessarily arbitrary about the word. Their appointment to stumble over the word is not the cause of disbelief. Rather disbelief is the cause of their appointment to stumble over the word.

Zion's Serving Patriots (2:9-10)

9—But ye are a chosen generation, a royal priesthood, a holy nation, a peculiar people; that ye should show forth the praises of him who hath called you out of darkness into his marvelous light:

10—Which in time past were not a people, but are now the people of God: which had not obtained mercy, but now have obtained mercy.

Zion's patriots are growing, committed and serving. Their service, delineated in verse 9 is predicated upon the spiritual proximity of the patriots to God.

Verse 9. Five declarations are featured which enlighten the reader concerning God's purposes with His people. First, God's people are a chosen people *(genos eklekton)*, that is, an elect offspring. *Genos* does not mean generation in the sense of people living within a certain time span. The word derives from the Greek verb *ginomai* which means "to be born." The emphasis is again upon relationship to the family of God. The second appellation is "royal priesthood." Here again the priesthood of the believer is the focus together with the famil- iar metaphor representing the Christian as royalty. Note that the evangelistic mandate involved with priesthood is particularly in view here, as demonstrated by the last phrase in the verse.

Further, men of faith constitute a holy nation. The point is that while geographical boundaries and racial similarities tend to demarcate the nations of the world, the pilgrim national entity is demarcated by holiness. "Peculiar people" is an interesting translation. The word "peculiar" should not be understood in terms of "oddity." Sadly, too many Christians would qualify neatly if that were the connotation. "Peculiar" translates *peripoiēsin,* a compound term inculcating *poieō,* meaning "to form" or "to make," and the preposition *peri,* meaning "around." Apparently the significance is that God's people are formed around Him. The purpose of all the above is to publish the virtues of the one who called us out of the darkness and into His glorious light.

"Show forth" is the King James Version rendering of a picturesque word *exangeilēte* which is formed from *angellō* ("to announce") and *ek* ("out"). The English term "evangelism" is derived from part of this word. Indeed, this is just another form of the word which carries much of the same idea. In all of the roles mentioned earlier in the verse, the follower of Christ is to be "announcing out" the virtues of the one who has called him out of darkness. The new state is one of marvelous light. The reference to "light" is an allusion to knowledge, understanding, and the absence of the works of darkness.

The importance of the concept is vivid to anyone who has risen in the night, having remembered that he failed to brush his teeth. Not wishing to awaken family, he attempts to negotiate the "familiar" terrain in darkness. Unaware that his toddler son left an iron truck full of marbles in the path or that the tube of toothpaste had been moved and a tube of hair-gel substituted, he proceeds to aching and distasteful disaster (to say nothing of the start to his slumbering family) simply because he did not accept the light. The author's experience of the above makes this passage especially significant, particularly the adjective "marvelous"!

Verse 10. This state of redemptive purpose has not always been the case. Once God's people were not a people. This does not imply lack of personhood. The emphasis is upon lack of unity, isolation from fellowship and purpose. That former status is history since they are now unified as a holy national entity of royal priests. Individually they had not formerly obtained mercy. The perfect participle here testifies to a continued state of being outside the mercies of God. Then God intervenes and they obtain mercy (aorist tense) indicating a conclusive act on the part of God.

Wars of the Soul

Author's Translation (2:11-25)

11—Beloved, I exhort [you] as strangers and pilgrims to abstain from fleshly desires, which continually wage war against the soul.

12—Maintaining your virtuous manner of life in the midst of the nations, so that in the thing which they are slandering you as evildoers, as a result of observing your good works they may glorify God in the day of inspection.

13—Be submissive to every human institution through the Lord; whether to a king as being superior,

14—or to governors as being sent by him for the punishment of the ones doing evil and for the praise of the ones doing good;

15—Because this is the will of God, [by] doing good to muzzle the ignorance of vain men.

16—[Live] as free men, yet not employing freedom as a cloak for evil, but as servants of God.

17—Honor all men, love the brotherhood, reverence God, honor the king.

18—Servants being submissive to masters in all reverence, not only to the good and kind, but also to the unreasonable.

19—For this is grace if because of conscience toward God one patiently endures grief when suffering unjustly.

20—For what credit [is there] if while sinning and being punished you endure? But if while doing good and suffering you should patiently endure, this is grace before God.

21—For unto this were you called, because Christ also suffered for you, leaving to you a pattern in order that you should follow in his tracks.

22—Who committed no sin, neither was there found deceit in His mouth;

23—Who being reviled, reviled not in return; while suffering he did not threaten, but continually committed [Himself] to the one who judges righteously;

24—Who Himself bore our sins in His body on the tree, so that while dying to sin we might be made alive to righteousness; by whose wounds you were healed.

25—For you were as sheep continually wandering astray, but now you have been converted to the shepherd and guardian of your souls.

The Enemies of the Soul (2:11-17)

11—Dearly beloved, I beseech you as strangers and pilgrims, abstain from fleshly lusts, which war against the soul;

12—Having your conversation honest among the Gentiles: that, whereas they speak against you as evildoers, they may by your good works, which they shall behold, glorify God in the day of visitation.

13—Submit yourselves to every ordinance of man for the Lord's sake: whether it be to the king, as supreme;

14—Or unto governors, as unto them that are sent by him for the punishment of evildoers, and for the praise of them that do well.

15—For so is the will of God, that with well doing ye may put to silence the ignorance of foolish men:

16—As free, and not using your liberty for a cloak of maliciousness, but as the servants of God.

17—Honor all men. Love the brotherhood. Fear God. Honor the King.

Paul frequently borrowed the language of conflict to describe the spiritual encounter with the minions of Satan. The classic passage is Ephesians 6:10-17, in which the apostle pictures the panoply of the saints. Peter also knows of that inner threat of confrontation where battles more strategic and far-reaching than most physical wars are a daily occurrence. Verses 11 to 17 discuss some of the enemies which assault the soul. Verses 18 through 20 focus on the attitude of saints under fire, while the remaining verses of the chapter present Christ as the example to follow.

Verse 11. "Beseech" is a translation of *parakalō* which literally means "to call to one's side." A fine translation would be "to give an invitation." The terminology properly belongs to the climax of an address. Having presented a proposition and its application, there follows an "invitation" or, as it is elsewhere rendered, "an exhortation." In this case the invitation is extended in the gentle and sweet demeanor of one who calls his listeners "beloved." The exhortation which follows is based on the nature of the relationship which Peter's hearers sustain to their world. In the first verse of the epistle, Peter called them "strangers" or "pilgrims." Now he employs that same word again (*parepidēmos*) and precedes it with still another descriptive term, *paroikos*.

Some authors suggest that the use of the two words is merely stylistic so that they should be understood as synonyms. In a recent commentary, John H. Elliott devotes an entire chapter to a demonstration of the significance of the terms, showing in the process that both words carry instructive nuances which aid in the understanding of First Peter. Elliott argues that *paroikos* should be translated "resident alien" and *parepidēmos* "visiting strangers."[1] Evidence from classical and extra-biblical Greek appears to sustain his claim. *Paroikos* literally means "beside the house," while *parepidēmos* means "beside the people." Both terms indicate temporary domicile. But, on the one hand, *paroikos* indicates residence which is not intended to be permanent, i.e., the residence of an alien who is on an official mission. *Parepidēmos*, on the other hand, indicates a relationship to the people themselves. The believer is *beside* the people, ministering in Christ's name, but never *among* the people in the sense of belonging to their unredeemed race.

---

[1]Elliott, *Home for the Homeless*, p. 47.

Because of this special relationship, the pilgrim is to abstain from fleshly desires which war against the soul. The precise nature of these fleshly desires is not the object of the present discussion. Instead Peter waits until later in the epistle (4:3) to list specifics. This present verse is intended to stress the effect of such desires upon the soul. Two emphases are notable. First, lust does wage war against the soul of a man. A believer lured into evil by lust loses his sense of the presence and power of God. Satan stirs up desires to attack the soul of a saint with the purpose of inflicting a wound that will severely restrict service to God. Second, it is not as much the body as it is the soul of man that endures these onslaughts. By soul, *psuchē*, Peter means the immaterial aspect of a man, the part of him that survives biological death. The soul is the spiritual battleground for man.

Verse 12. "Conversation" means much more than "talk." *Anastophē* evolved from *strephō* which meant originally "to steer" and referred to the work of a helmsman on a ship. The word eventually came to mean "turn." Coupled with the *ana*, which means "again," the idea of a "turn to a new direction" was established. The direction which the believer's life has turned is to be "honest" (*kalos*), an adjective which is translated in numerous ways ranging from "honest" to "good," "beautiful," "profitable," "honorable," or "virtuous," as we have translated. "Virtuous" may come nearest to capturing the significance of the word as it is used here.

This virtuous conduct should be the saint's posture among the nations so that his very life-style becomes its own refutation of the allegation of men who accuse the believers of evil. For example, Henry Bullinger's malicious attack upon the Anabaptists of the Reformation is punctuated by praise of their goodness. Bullinger wrote,

> Those who unite with them will by their ministers be received into their church by rebaptism and repentance and newness of life. They henceforth lead their lives under a semblance of quiet

spiritual conduct. They denounce covetousness, pride, profanity, the lewd conversation and immorality of the world, the drinking and the gluttony. In fine, their hypocrisy is great and manifold.[2]

"Behold" is from *epopteuō* and means more than a cursory glance. The word was used in the vocabulary of the Greek mysteries where the *epopt* designated one who had attained the ultimate grade of initiation and was thereby admitted "to gaze upon" sacred things.[3] This picturesque term suggests continued observation of the good works of believers to the end that God is glorified in the day of visitation or, as I have translated, the day of "inspection." "Visitation" translates *episkopē*, a word which is often rendered "bishop." The basic meaning of "overseer" helps in this passage to capture the sense in that a day will come when God will "oversee," "inspect," or "visit" His people. Their good works will not only convince the world's critics but also will redound to the glory of God in the day when God visits among His people.

Verse 13. "Submit" is a military term describing the response of a junior officer to the command of a senior officer. The word has the connotation of volunteering rather than being constrained. The motivation for this activity arises neither from the ordinance nor from the king but rather out of a desire to please God. "Ordinance" (*ktisis*) is usually rendered "creation." The reference here is to foundational statutes created by human governments to control evil in society. Under no circumstance should the mandate be construed to include submission to any law of man which is in violation of a command of God. As Francis Schaeffer says,

> If there is no final place for civil disobedience, then the government has been made autonomous, and as such, it has been put in the place of the Living God.[4]

---

[2]Leonard Verduin, *The Reformers and Their Stepchildren*, p. 110.
[3]Bigg, *Commentary on St. Peter and St. Jude*, p. 138.
[4]Francis Schaeffer, *A Christian Manifesto*, p. 130.

Verse 14. Verse 13 specifies submission to kings and verse 14 adds governors (*hēgemonon*), a word which gives us our English word hegemony. The reference is probably to Roman provincial governors, whose primary task is outlined in the verse. They are to punish evildoers and to praise those that do well. "Punish" is *ekdikēsis* which combines the word for "justice" with the preposition meaning "out of." Hence, out of justice retributive action is to be taken by governors. Such language not only argues for the administering of punishment for evil deeds in society but also conditions that punishment by specifying that it should arise out of justice.

Romans 13:1-7 features Paul's more extensive development of the same theme. The reference to the "bearing of the sword" implies the use of capital punishment when necessary (see Gen. 9:6). Again, however, it must be stressed that there may come a time when civil disobedience is necessary. When necessary, one must be prepared to accept the full consequences of his act. Furthermore, that expedient is never in order unless the ordinances of constituted authorities call for the violation or disestablishment of God's ordinances. As long as magistrates follow the expressed purpose delineated herein, they are serving as ministers of God. Furthermore, while powers of kings and governors may indeed exceed those specified here, great expansion of that authority almost inevitably works ill for society. The basic reason for all government must remain the restraint and punishment of evil and the reward or praise of those who do good.

Verse 15. With God the weapons of warfare are not carnal. Following the announced theme of spiritual warfare with lust, Peter argues that the enemy will be defeated by the irresistible display of good works. This is the will of God. Furthermore, it will silence the ignorance of foolish men. That last observation is pregnant with significance. "Silence" is a word which is more vividly translated "muzzle."

"Ignorance" is *agnōsia*, which gives us the English word "agnostic," one who pleads ignorance. Literally the word employs the alpha negative with *gnōsis*, the word meaning "knowledge," to indicate the absence of knowledge.

Several Greek words usually translated "foolish" are by-passed in favor of *aphrōn* in this text. Peter's term "foolish men" is the same one used in Luke 12:20 to describe the rich farmer whose only thought was the building of new and greater barns. The derivation of the word is fascinating. *Phrēn* actually meant "diaphragm." With the alpha negative particle attached, the word meant "no diaphragm." Gradually the word evolved, coming to mean "mind" or "intellect." Apparently this happened when the word was used in the way the English expression is employed when someone remarks, "He has no intestinal fortitude." In any case, the point is that mindless, ignorant men who, failing to understand love for Jesus, level verbal barrages against the believer, find it increasingly difficult to maintain those assaults when the response of the believer is only good works.

The advice offered here is precisely the same as Paul's in Romans 12:19-20. Paul suggests that vengeance belongs only to God. Consequently we are to feed a hungry enemy and thus "heap coals of fire on his head." That phrase has often been misconstrued. Some see the coals of fire as punishment for the enemy. The opposite is the case, as verse 21 confirms by stressing that evil is to be overcome with good. The "coals of fire" represent the awakening of conscience on the part of the enemy. The result will often be what Peter envisions: the ignorance of foolish men will be muzzled.

Verse 16. In two distinct but not unrelated spheres, this verse assumes a position of importance disproportionate to the scant attention which it has received. Both doctrine and ethics are touched by the poignant insight provided by Peter. The fact of Christian liberty is acknowledged. This assertion is made against the backdrop of almost certain slavery for some of those to whom the letter would be read. In the author's translation, the word "live" has been added, indicating our belief that this verb was understood by writer and reader. The astonishing declaration then advises men, some of whom are slaves, to live as free men.

On the other hand, the emphasis of the verse is not on freedom but on the misuse of freedom. Peter's concern is that some may substitute license for liberty. Peter knew that responsible liberty was a wonderful and productive posture. He also knew that the selfish exercise of liberty quickly degenerates to anarchy. Therefore, he cautions that while we live as free men, we are never to avail ourselves of that liberty to use it as a "cloak of maliciousness."

"Cloak" derives from *epikalumma*, the verb form of which means "to cover over." The picture presented is literally one of "cloak and dagger." The cloak hides the dagger, the instrument of terror, under a garment of respectability.

"Maliciousness" is the King James Version rendering of *kakia*. This is one of those Greek words which carries a remarkable assortment of meanings. Basically the concept is that of "evil." Shades of meanings include maliciousness, wickedness, depravity, malignity, worthlessness, and corruption. In this instance, Peter probably drafted a word with such latitude on purpose. He likely intended to suggest that freedom can be used as a cloak for all of the things *kakia* might represent.

Generally, there are two broad areas of applicability to modernity. First, congregations that emphasize the doctrines of grace often come perilously close to making those doctrines a cloak for evil. The insistence upon the security of the believer in Christ, while scriptural, may in the minds of some become a security that spawns carelessness. Furthermore, reaction in such communions to pharisaic legalism may produce arguments such as, "In Christ, I am not bound by the law." But such positions utterly misconstrue the doctrine of Christian liberty, making it a cloak for evils of the fleshly nature. As Jesus cogently demonstrated, His own principles begin at the limits of the law and extend beyond them.

Whereas the law dealt heavily in actions, the principles of Christ demand that proper attitudes and motivations serve as foundations for right actions.

A second arena of Christian liberty is one mentioned in the previous chapter—the priesthood of all believers. Those who distort this doctrine argue that as a Christian one has the right to believe whatever he wishes. This is not at all what the doctrine of the priesthood of believers teaches When thus fashioned, a profound liberty may become a cloak which secludes from view a wicked heart in rebellion against God. Particularly is this true when freedom means the license to reject the truthfulness of what is recorded in the Bible. In Second Peter 3:16 the apostle speaks of the unlearned and unstable who "wrest" the Scriptures. "Wrest" is *streblousin*, which literally means "to twist" or "to distort."

Verse 17. A summary verse for this section precedes the final discussion of chapter 2 in which Christ's own sufferings are presented as a flawless example. Four rather inclusive relationships are advocated.

(1) Honor all men.
(2) Love the brotherhood.
(3) Fear God.
(4) Honor the king.

This approach suggests that there are at least four levels upon which the believer is to function as a pilgrim example.

(1) The entire human family.
(2) The Church of the Lord.
(3) God.
(4) Government officials whose roles are ordained of God.

While the concepts enjoined are self-explanatory, two interesting phenomena should be noted. First, the same word is used for the attitude of the saints toward kings as for their attitude toward all men. The only difference is that the first imperative translated "honor" is an aorist imperative, while the second is a present imperative. The aorist imperative differs only in that it views the action mandated as a perpetual state of affairs. Now the key in the use of the same word demanding "honor" for kings and for all men is not that kings were to be treated as ordinary men, but rather that ordinary men were to be treated as kings.

The second significant phenomenon concerns the graduated importance of the various mandates.

(1) Kings and all men are to be honored *(timaō)*.

(2) The brotherhood (other believers) are to be loved *(agapaō)*.

(3) God is to be feared *(phobeomai)*.

All three words are weighty concepts. But whereas *timaō* means "to treasure," there are many treasures which one might treat very carefully, yet still be unwilling to love sacrificially. Therefore, the command to love *(agapaō*, which means selfless giving in behalf of another's well-being) is a more demanding admonition than the mandate "to honor." Even beyond those commands is the prescribed "fear" or "reverence" for God. This is not a shrinking, quaking horror. What is enjoined upon the believer is a recognition of the exalted holiness of God. The nearest human approximation would be the fear of a mischievous little boy who nearly worships his father. While he adores his father, he knows that his own behavior may be the occasion for punishment at his father's hand.

Until this day, this reverence or fear is in my own heart toward my father. As maturation progressed, fear of his physical punishment subsided. But that fear was replaced by the fear of his displeasure. Because I love him and honor him as the greatest man I ever knew, I never want to hurt him. Yet, I do not therefore avoid him. To the contrary, I covet his presence and attention. Mature Christian fear of God is of a similar stripe. Though His chastisement can be severe, it is the possibility of causing Him displeasure that we fear. Peter commands, "fear God."

The Equanimity of the Sufferer (2:18-20)

18—Servants, be subject to your masters with all fear; not only to the good and gentle, but also to the froward.

19—For this is thankworthy, if a man for conscience toward God endure grief, suffering wrongfully.

20—For what glory is it, if, when ye be buffeted for your faults, ye shall take it patiently? but if, when ye do well, and suffer for it, ye take it patiently, this is acceptable with God.

Verse 18. Equanimity, or evenness of temper, is now asked of servants. As indicated above, many of the first-century readers of this epistle would be slaves since nearly half of the Roman Empire was of that status. However, the verses are equally applicable to circumstances in which men are responsible to others. This could include employer-employee, magistrate-citizen, or pastor-flock. When viewed in this way, the verses have relevance even in a society where fortunately slavery is non-existent.

Several different words are translated "servant" in Greek. *Hupēretēs* is translated "ministers" in First Corinthians 4:1. The word means "under-rower" and referred to a galley slave rowing in the lowest of the ship's galleys. The most frequently occurring term in the New Testament is *doulos*. This word is a general term to describe all varieties of slavery. Two words specify domestic responsibilities but differ in rank assignment. *Oiketēs* refers to a common household servant, while *oikonomos* refers to the manager of the household. This word was sometimes used of slaves and on occasion of hired hands. Finally, some slaves reached the exalted position of *paidagōgos*, one to whom the children of aristocrats were assigned for rearing and tutoring. Paul says that the law is our *paidagōgos* to bring us to Jesus.

The slave alluded to by Peter is the *oiketēs*, a common household servant. He is instructed to submit with all reverence *(phobos)* to the masters. "Masters" is *despotais*, which gives us our English word "despot." However, the negative image of the English word "despot" was not naturally associated with the Greek term. That some *despotais* were worthy of all the repugnance associated with the English word is apparent in Peter's challenge for submission to the "froward" as well as to the good and gentle. "Froward" translates *skoliois* which may mean "crooked," "tortuous," "wicked," or "morose," but always implies "unreasonable." Regardless of the reason for this unreasonableness and the form it acquires, the servant is to be submissive just as if his *despotais* were "good" and "gentle." "Good" translates *agathos* while "gentle" is *epieikēs*. "Virtuous" and "kind" would be good translations also.

Verse 19. The rationale for this conduct enjoined in verse 18 is now explained in verse 19. "Thankworthy" is an odd, though not incorrect, translation of *charis,* the word usually translated "grace." Of course, the point of the word concerns an unexpected and undeserved favor. Obviously unreasonable masters could not expect submissiveness and non-retaliation from abused servants. Nevertheless, the Christian servant must exhibit such behavior as a matter of grace. This is done in turn because of his conscience toward God. In verses 21-25 the sufferings of Christ in our behalf are chronicled. If Christ endured so much at the hands of sinners and did so without retaliation, how could one in good conscience before God do otherwise than to follow His example?

"Endure" is a vivid Greek verb, *hupopherō*. Literally it means "to bear under" or "to bear on one's shoulders" a heavy burden. Peter recognizes that these situations produce pain and that such suffering is unjust. Nevertheless, the demand is not softened. It is further elucidated.

Verse 20. The contrast presented by Peter is one which recognizes certain inevitabilities. Because of sin, one is going to suffer. The question then becomes, will one suffer justly, hardly a circumstance in which credit would be allowed, or will one suffer unjustly. If the case is one of unjust suffering, then one may, with proper attitudes, gain the smile of God in the matter. The word "glory" is not *doxa*, which we usually find, but *kleos*, which may be translated "rumor," "report," or better here, "credit." "Buffet" is the Greek word *kolaphizō* and means "to beat harshly and repeatedly." Credit accrues to the account of the believer when he endures such beatings provided he has not deserved them.

What kind of credit goes to the believer who patiently endures such unjust scourgings? The King James Version says this endurance is "acceptable" with God. But the word is *charis* again, the same word which was translated "thankworthy" in verse 19. The idea seems to be that God delights in and even rewards the exercise of grace in the believer's life since such examples point to the grace of God.

The Example of the Savior (2:21-25)

21—For even hereunto were ye called: because Christ also suffered for us, leaving us an example, that ye should follow his steps:

22—Who did no sin, neither was guile found in his mouth:

23—Who, when he was reviled, reviled not again; when he suffered, he threatened not; but committed himself to him that judgeth righteously:

24—Who his own self bare our sins in his own body on the tree, that we, being dead to sins, should live unto righteousness: by whose stripes ye were healed.

25l—For ye were as sheep going astray; but are now returned unto the Shepherd and Bishop of your souls.

Verse 21. Earlier verses have noted the enemies of the soul and the equanimity of the sufferer. The final verses of the chapter focus on the example of the Savior. In fact, verse 21 begins by stating the ultimate reason for this patient conduct. It is not just a matter of grace in the believer's heart or of credit before God. The major reason is that believers have been called to this kind of behavior. The calling is not only explicit in the written word but implicit in the example of the Living Word. Christ suffered for us, leaving us an example which we should follow.

The expression "suffered for us" in the better manuscripts of the New Testament is "suffered for you." Here is a classic

[*95*]

case that anyone can grasp in the science of textual criticism and the reliability of the text of Scripture. Did the autograph of Peter say that Christ suffered for "us" or for "you?" In Greek the difference is slight. "You" is *humōn*, "us" is *hēmōn*—only one vowel's difference. The manuscript evidence is numerically about half for one reading and half for the other. However, the older and more reliable texts noticeably favor the reading "suffered for you." We can, therefore, in spite of textual variants, be reasonably sure that Peter wrote "suffered for you." The critical question concerns the theological effect. In other words, does it matter which reading is correct as far as the teaching of the text is concerned? The answer is an emphatic "no." Christ died for you. It is also made abundantly clear that He died for us. Only one reading was in the inerrant autograph, but either statement leaves the theology intact. Such is the case with other such variant readings. None of the other undecided readings will alter the basic theology. You can trust your Bible!

This is also a case in which the preposition "for" assumes profound exegetical importance. The word is *huper*. The term frequently carries the thought of substitution. This may be observed in Philemon 13 where Paul says he would have retained Onesimus that the slave might have ministered to Paul "for" (*huper*) Philemon. That is, since Philemon could not be there to help, Onesimus might minister in his place. Similar instances occur in John 10:11 where the good shepherd gives his life "for" (*huper*) the sheep. Again in John 11:50 Caiaphas argues better than he knew that one must die "for" (*huper*) the people.[5]

No amount of theological gymnastics can obviate the clear meaning of this statement. Christ died in our place. His death was substitutionary in character. The Scriptures declare, "The wages of sin is death." The death of Jesus involved one who

---

[5]For an excellent discussion of the significance of *huper*, see Leon Morris, *The Apostolic Preaching of the Cross*, p. 59.

was innocent of any sin. He died in order to satisfy the just demands of a Holy God against sin. In this He died in our stead.

But His death provided not only our salvation, but also our example. Peter now uses two words which are found nowhere else in the Greek New Testament and are even rare in other ancient Greek literature. "Leaving" is *hupolimpanō*, which is used to describe that which remains of an unpaid balance. "Example" is *hupogrammos* which refers literally to something which has been traced or signed. Hence the vivid picture of the atonement of Jesus is seen not only as a satisfaction of the just wrath of God against sin but also as an example left permanently with us so that over His example we may lay our own lives, tracing the pattern of our lives by the abiding example of His life. The fact that Peter used two such unusual words not only indicates the intellectual progress of the fisherman apostle but also strongly suggests the matter of the "verbal inspiration" of the sacred text.

Verse 22. The sinlessness of Jesus is avowed in two major areas—actions and utterances. Isaiah 53:9 is the Old Testament source of appeal. The sinlessness of Jesus in general is assumed. The relevance of this claim relates expressly to the suffering of Jesus. This is the case in two different respects. First, it is the sinlessness of Jesus that enables His atoning death to be efficacious for sinners. Second, Jesus, under the ultimate pressures to which men may be subject, remained free of overt sin or even retaliatory word. Illegal trial, misrepresentation of motives, physical abuse, slander, scourging, crucifixion, and derisive mocking all failed to draw from Jesus either action or word that could be called sinful.

Verse 23. The indignities which pierced Jesus most deeply are now recounted by Peter. When men reviled Him, He prayed for their forgiveness. While He suffered, He did not resort to threatening—the almost universal human response. Most who suffer at the hands of others offer threats in order to intimidate and force a retreat on the part of the persecutor.

The reason for Christ's behavior was that He had made a total commitment to Him who judges righteously. This affirmation by Peter is important because it demonstrates Jesus' determination not to be shaped by the circumstances of the moment but rather to be molded by the will of His Father. Furthermore, Jesus thus affirmed His own confidence in the righteous providence of God the Father. What men said did not ultimately matter. What God thought would be the last word. He was content to await righteous judgment at the hands of the Father.

Verse 24. The nature of the atonement is primarily that of substitution. Having emphasized the moral example which Christ provided, Peter carefully returns to the vicarious nature of the cross. It is almost as if he anticipated the era when some theologians would become uncomfortable with the concept of God's wrath and hence of the necessity of a substitutionary atonement. To avoid misunderstanding, Peter now returns to the essence of the death of Christ. He declares that Jesus bore our sins in His own body on the cross. The verb "bore" is a translation of *anēnenken*, an aorist active form of *anapherō* which literally means "to bear up." The aorist tense views the action of Christ as a whole and hints at its accomplishment in one act. That Christ "bore up" our sins is surely to indicate that those iniquities were laid upon one who was innocent. If the substitutionary nature of the Atonement is to be doubted, it cannot be doubted on the basis of Scripture. Only the presupposition that God could not be a God of wrath spawns such unscriptural theory.

The result of Christ's vicarious sacrifice is a miraculous transformation of human life. The fisherman suggests that when Christ bore our sins, His act made it possible for us to die to the consequences and to the enslaving power of sin. He does not suggest that the saved no longer sin. He does indicate that there has been a death to the power and consequences of that sin. The saint no longer faces spiritual death (Rom. 6:23) because Jesus paid the wages of sin completely.

The death of Jesus somehow breaks the power of sin in the life of the Christian so that he is able to live righteously before God. In other words, there are two miracles. Christ's death is one in which He accepted the judgment of God against sin on the tree. Furthermore, when the Holy Spirit applies the efficacy of that death to the soul of the believer, a change is wrought which instills in the disciple a love for righteousness.

Finally, Peter quotes a line from Isaiah 53:5, "by whose stripes we are healed." This is fortuitous since many have attempted to employ this avowal as a proof text, arguing that God must will to heal all physical maladies in His children because He had already suffered in the body on the cross. But Peter's use of the quote is clearly in the context of the redemption of the soul. The healing thus specified is the new birth or regeneration.

Verse 25. The new attitude of a converted man engendering in him a desire for righteousness is now contrasted with the former posture. Before the experience of salvation, the recipients of Peter's letter were as sheep continually straying. "Were" is an imperfect form of the verb "to be." The imperfect tense suggests continual action in past time. "Going astray" is, on the other hand, a present passive participle. The present tense also indicates uninterrupted action. In other words, before conversion they were in a constant state of continually becoming lost, always straying away. The metaphor of a hopelessly recalcitrant sheep, unaware of its precarious circumstance, perpetually wandering into greater lostness is a vivid picture.

The metaphor of the lost sheep, which Peter had doubtless learned from the witness of His Lord, is continued in the last phrase of the verse. Christians have "turned again" or "returned" to the Shepherd. The Shepherd is the Good Shepherd, as Jesus had identified Himself. His shepherdly task is that of a bishop. We began this chapter by entitling it the "Wars of the Soul." We conclude the chapter with the Bishop of the soul. The answer to the wars of the soul rests with the Bishop of our souls. "Bishop" is *episkopos*. *Skopos* was loaned to English as our word "scope." It appears in such words as "microscope," "telescope," and "stethoscope". The basic sense is that of close observation. The preposition *epi* is affixed to the beginning of the word and means "over." Hence the Bishop is one who carefully "oversees" His flock.

Note that the "souls" of the saints are the objects of this oversight. This does not indicate lack of concern for the physical life of the believer. It does illustrate vividly the truth made evident everywhere in Scripture. The spiritual well-being of man, including his eternal circumstances, are much more important to God than are changing, temporal physical circumstances. Religion, theology, and ecclesiology must always devote themselves primarily to the eternal concerns of the souls of the people and secondarily to temporal circumstances in the physical world.

Domestic Delight

1. Elegance God Honors (3:1-4)
2. Examples Men Honor (3:5-6)
3. Expressions Women Honor (3:7)

Author's Translation (3:1-7)

1—In the same way wives be submissive to your own husbands so that even if any [of them] are disobedient to the word, they shall be won without a word through the conduct of their wives.

2—As they observe the purity of your conduct in fear

3—Of whom let it not be the outward embellishments of the braiding of hair and the wearing of gold or putting on of garments,

4—But the concealed man of the heart, in the incorruptible gentle and quiet spirit, which is much treasured before God.

5—For in this way formerly even the holy women, the ones continually hoping in God, adorned themselves, being submissive to their own husbands.

6—As Sarah submitted to Abraham, calling him Lord; whose children you have become, doing good and not being frightened by any dismay.

7—The husbands, in the same way, making your home together according to knowledge, as [with] the more fragile vessel bestowing honor to the woman, as also being co-heirs of the grace of life, in order that your prayers be not cut off.

Titus
2:5

Elegance God Honors (3:1-4)

1—Likewise, ye wives, be in subjection to your own husbands; that if any obey not the word, they also may without the word be won by the conversation of the wives;

2—While they behold your chaste conversation coupled with fear.

3—Whose adorning let it not be that outward adorning of plaiting the hair, and of wearing of gold, or of putting on of apparel;

4—But let it be the hidden man of the heart, in that which is not corruptible, even the ornament of a meek and quiet spirit, which is in the sight of God of great price.

The chapter break here is artificial. Having discussed proper responses of servants to masters, the discussion proceeds naturally to the more essential social unit, the family. The absence of a discussion of parent-child relationships does not suggest that such is unimportant. Peter knew that wholesome interchange between husband and wife creates an earthly environment in which other relationships tend to develop, reflecting the impact of the spouse relationship. He first discusses the nature of feminine beauty in verses 1-4, a section we have called "Elegance God Honors." Then in verses 5-6 we examine the gracious women of biblical history in "Examples Men Honor." Finally, verse 7 rehearses "Expressions Women Honor," an explication of the role of a believing husband.

Verse 1. "Submission" is the identical term employed in 2:18 to describe the actions of servants as they relate to their masters. This is fortuitous, especially in the light of misunderstandings of evangelical perspectives in the present supercharged feminist atmosphere. Under no circumstances is it possible to argue that Peter viewed servants as inferior to masters in any sense. In Philemon, Paul's treatment of Onesimus as a brother is once again the best insight into early Christian persuasion. Nevertheless, Peter recognizes not only conditions that do in fact exist in society but also an order which must exist in the home. Subordination of wife to husband is a subordination of office and not in any way inferiority of gender or person.

The critical importance of this concept is best demonstrated in the life of Jesus. In John 10:30 Jesus says plainly, "I and my Father are one." That is an unmistakable claim for the full deity of the Son as is indicated by the objection of the Jews in John 10:33 when they accused Jesus of blasphemy for making Himself God. On the other hand, that same Jesus said, "My Father is greater than I" (John 14:28). Is this a contradiction? Only a man determined to misconstrue could miss the obvious. Jesus is speaking of what He is in John 10:30—the Father and the Son fully share (with the Holy Spirit) *one* divine nature. In John 14:28 He is speaking of His official mission as the second Person of the Trinity in human flesh, of which Paul says He humbled Himself and "became obedient unto the death of the cross" (Phil. 2:8).

Now if Jesus is co-equal with the Father, yet voluntarily pours Himself into humanity (see Phil. 2:7), temporarily accepting a subordinate role of obedience to His Father in order to accomplish redemption, then how can submission to role subordination advocated in the Scriptures in other areas of our own lives be interpreted as demeaning? To reject such role assignments is to insist, as some are now attempting, that children should be virtually free from parental decision, since they, too, are fully human and should not be victimized by discrimination. But parents are instructed in the Scriptures to correct and discipline children who are to be subordinate in role assignments. The child may regard his life as far more renowned than the father's, but as a child, he is subject to the authority of his father. If he learns godly attitudes toward the various authorities to which he must relate as a youth, it is much more likely that he will respond to God as he ought.

Studying the model of the Trinity assists the believer in interpreting these verses and others like them in the Bible. In no sense are wives inferior to their husbands. Adam bore testimony to this when he said of Eve, "This is now bone of my bone, and flesh of my flesh" (Gen. 2:23). She is like him. Nevertheless, role assignments guaranteeing domestic order are clearly provided early in the Bible and equally sustained by other passages covering at least fifteen hundred years of written revelation. Therefore, it remains God's mandate to wives that upon choosing marriage, they voluntarily subordinate themselves to their own husbands.

Apparently, women were well represented in the churches of the geographical entities addressed by Peter. At least, there were women in the churches whose husbands were not saved. Naturally, any woman who genuinely cherishes her husband would be grieved at his condition of lostness. Even a kind of "holy anxiety" might be present. Peter anticipates the question, "How then do I reach my husband for Christ?" The answer shows that in this one instance the fisherman-apostle believed that conduct was more effective than verbal pressure. The sweet and gentle submission of godly wives will be so compelling that eventually husbands will be led to embrace Christ, even without verbal pleadings.

The husbands in question are described as those who "obey not the word." The word thus translated is *apeitheō* which is often rendered "unbelief." The only possible translation improvement which might reflect the strength of the word here is to translate the term "disobedient." These are men who are refusing to be obedient to the word. This is helpful because it suggests that these husbands know the word but have thus far chosen disobedience. Now if the wife demonstrates the effects of regeneration in her submissiveness to her own husband, the latter cannot resist the argument of a changed life.

"They may be won" is more definite in the Greek text. The mood is the indicative mood—the mood of reality—rather than subjunctive—the mood of potentiality—as it seems in the King James Version translation. The tense is future. Thus the better translation is "they also shall be won." The word "won" is itself interesting. *Kerdainō* means "to acquire possession." Apparently the word, which often had connotations of "profit by unfair advantage" in classical Greek, was another of those words which the early church fashioned to its own use.[1] This new sense is the way Peter uses the word here. The husbands are "acquired" for Christ.

Paul used the identical word five times in First Corinthians 9:19-22. There he speaks of gaining the more, gaining the Jews, etc. Exactly what he means by the five uses of this word "gain" is apparent in verse 22 since the last phrase says, "that I might by all means save some." "Save" is *sōzō* in Greek, the usual word meaning spiritual salvation. From these two instances of *kerdainō* it can be gleaned that the word was common ecclesiastical currency to describe the bringing of the lost to Christ.

One additional insight may prove helpful. This same word, with the word *aiskros* prefixed is the word which the King James Version translators usually rendered "filthy lucre" as in First Peter 5:2. *Kerdos*, which means "gain," is thus coupled with *aiskros*, meaning "dishonorable" or even "indecent." The concept of *kerdainō* then is "to gain" or "to win" for Christ, for fellowship, and for family who is estranged from Christ.

Verse 2. Precise aspects of this influential conduct are now provided. "Conduct" again is *anastophē*. This time, however, the word is accentuated with the addition of the adjective *hagnē*, meaning "pure" or "chaste." This pure conduct is also coupled with fear or reverence for God. Husbands will "behold" that conduct. "Behold" translates *epopteuō*, the same term which Peter used previously in 2:12 (see p. 87 in chap. 4 for analysis). Peter's fondness for this word in place of more conventional expressions is notable. The emphasis here, as in verse 12, is not upon seeing as such but upon careful observation.

Herein is a key. No one observes behavior at a more basic level than those in one's own house. All hypocrisy tends to vanish in the presence of those with whom we feel most at

---

[1]Liddell and Scott, *Greek-English Lexicon*, p. 942.

ease. Unbelieving husbands will find consistency of Christlike behavior more unanswerable than the finest honed intellectual apology or the most profound moral or emotional appeal. A radically altered life-style accentuated by an optimistic, confident, and happy demeanor will be a devastating blow against the finest worldly alternative.

Verse 3. Philosophers debated the nature of true beauty for two millennia. Peter now moves the discussion to aesthetics, disallowing the conventional concepts of beauty in favor of a godly perspective. Disallowed are coiffures, jewelry, and apparel. But these are not rejected per se. They are rejected as being the repositories of true beauty. This last point is crucial. If this passage and First Timothy 2:9 are to be construed as a prohibition of the use of jewelry and the preparation of the hair, then two serious problems arise. First, the wearing of apparel is mentioned. Surely Peter is not prohibiting that! Second, Sarah is cited in verse 6 as a godly woman. While the Bible makes no mention of Sarah's wearing jewelry, Abraham's servant is sent to find a wife for Isaac. He goes laden with gifts which included jewelry. Upon arriving in Mesopotamia, Rebekah is located and promptly endowed with a golden earring and two bracelets for her hands (Gen. 24:22). Coupled with a reading of books like Esther and Song of Solomon, the truth emerges that holy women "in the old time" (v. 5) certainly did adorn themselves with gold and expensive apparel and doubtless were not clones as far as their hair was concerned.

Peter does not forbid any of the above. He simply insists that the measure of a woman's beauty is never to be found in such accouterments. "Adorning" is the Greek word *kosmos* which is also frequently translated "world." Basically, the idea is that of decoration or ornamentation. Perhaps the word came to mean "world" in the sense that the world or the universe is the adornment of decoration which God has given. This perhaps is the sense of Psalm 19:1, "The heavens declare the glory of God; and the firmament showeth his handiwork."

Concerning the "plaiting of the hair" Bigg comments that "it was an art highly cultivated by Greek and Roman ladies."[2] "Wearing" of gold is *peritheseōs*, from a verb meaning "to place" and the preposition "around." "Putting on" of apparel is *enduseōs*, from *duō* which means "to sink" and *ev* which means "in." Thus the meaning is literally to "sink into" clothes. The *locus classicus* for the abuse of these adornments is in Isaiah's satire on the women of Jerusalem (see Is. 3:18-24). Isaiah speaks of women whose attitudes were so repulsive that their only beauty was in their adornment.

Verse 4. Genuine beauty is internal rather than ornamental. Internal beauty will be reflected externally in attitudes, actions, and even facial expressions. It can be enhanced very little by such accouterments as those mentioned in verse 3. Ostentation in adornment may actually detract from true beauty or merely reflect the total absence of the latter. By the "hidden man of the heart" Peter indicates that the beauty of the spiritual man is of greater consequence than that of the physical frame. This is true for several obvious reasons. First, physical beauty is always subject to decadence with the passing of years. Furthermore, even the most beautiful may fracture their own appearance through a vitriolic spirit. By contrast, the beauty of the "hidden man," that is, of the recesses of the heart, tends to increase with growing spiritual maturity.

More specifically, the qualities which the Lord calls beautiful are "not corruptible." This is the identical word Peter chose in 1:4 to describe the inheritance of the believer. Two such imperishable features of spirit are specified for godly women, namely, a "meek and quiet spirit." A loud and boisterous woman is distasteful to all, a misfit in any company.

---

[2]Bigg, *Commentary on St. Peter and St. Jude,* p. 152.

Regardless of her physical loveliness, the tendency is not to trust her or seek her company. On the other hand, a woman who moves with quiet dignity and gentleness has an appeal which renders her physical blemishes unimportant.

The two words to describe this beauty in spirit are *praeōs* and *hēsukia*, "gentleness" and "quietness." *Praeōs* may mean "meek," "kind," "benevolent," or "gentle." The basic idea seems to be gentleness. The word was frequently used to describe a fierce animal that had been tamed or a horse that had been broken. The comment seems to suggest an acquired rather than natural characteristic.

"Quietness," or *hēsukia*, is an important term that must not be interpreted to mean "total silence." The best way to grasp the meaning, perhaps, is to contrast *hēsukia* with *sigē*, another word meaning "silence." In First Corinthians 14:34 Paul tells women to remain silent *(sigatōsan)* in the churches. In First Timothy 2:11, the same apostle counsels that women learn in silence *(hēsukia)*. The word used in First Corinthians means absolute silence, while *hēsukia* in First Timothy represents an attitude of general self-control and meekness. The subject in First Corinthians 14 is the abuse of spiritual gifts with special emphasis on the gift of tongues. Women are forbidden by Paul to speak in tongues in the churches. Not a syllable is allowable. The concept of *hēsukia* does not forbid speech. It does not even preclude teaching. It does mandate that a meek and quiet spirit should prevail among godly women.

A gentle and quiet spirit is "of great price" in the sight of God. The vivid Greek word *polutelēs* is the term employed. This word is a compound word uniting *polus*, which means "much" or "great," with *telos* which may mean "end," "consummation," or "fulfillment." The idea bound up in the word seems to be that a gentle and quiet spirit is the goal of genuine beauty which every woman ought to seek. Before God the development of that spirit is "much consummation" for any woman. It is an ultimate achievement. Hence God greatly values that quality in any woman.

Examples Men Honor (3:5-6)

5—For after this manner in the old time the holy women also, who trusted in God, adorned themselves, being in subjection unto their own husbands:

6—Even as Sarah obeyed Abraham, calling him lord: whose daughters ye are, as long as ye do well, and are not afraid with any amazement.

Verse 5. Having pinpointed the nature of the elegance that God honors, Peter now appeals to the Old Testament for examples men honor. Only one is given by name, but others are alluded to in a general way. The appeal to holy women of old is presented first. "Of old" is a translation of *pote*, which simply means "formerly." This is not an appeal to the good old days—just the citation of known examples from the past. These holy women are said to have "trusted" in God. The translation is accurate even though the word thus translated is not the usual word for "faith" or "trust." In fact, *elpizō* is normally given as "hope." The concept is again not a vague hope but a confident expectation. Sometimes the idea of "repose" is involved. These nuances of the word doubtless led the King James Version translators to render the term "trusted." These holy women qualify as examples because they adorned themselves (*kosmeō*) with gentle and quiet spirits, exhibiting submissiveness to their own husbands. That they are called "holy women" is a reminder that this "adorning" developed as a result of a prior commitment to the will and purpose of God.

Verse 6. The general example having been provided, a specific, well-known figure is now offered. Sarah "obeyed" Abraham, even calling him "lord." "Obeyed" is *hupēkousen* which combines the preposition *hupo* which means "under," and *akouō* which is translated "to hear." The verb suggests that obedience is an act of hearing oneself "under" or "into submission." This involves some understanding. The comprehension necessary is a grasp of role assignment. Sarah, understanding her position as Abraham's wife, hears his requests and molds her responses in obedience. This approach is foreign to the dictator-subject approach that some erroneously suggest exists in the Bible.

Sarah even called Abraham "lord." Again this was Sarah's choice of terminology, not one brutally coerced upon her. The reference is evidently an appeal to Genesis 18:12. In that text the angel has just announced to Abraham the coming birth of a son. Sarah laughs, questioning the possibility of one as advanced in age as she giving birth, especially since her "lord" was advanced in years also. The word "lord" is *kurios* which came into Latin as "Caesar" and into German as "kaiser." Though the term is often used of Jesus, the word itself does not necessarily imply deity. Basic to the concept is the idea of "owner" or "master." The same is true of the Hebrew *adonai*, which is found in Genesis 18:12.

Furthermore, the word order in Greek is emphatic. The order reads this way in the autograph, "lord him continually calling." The word "lord" appears first, emphasizing the vigorous avowal. The present participle, "calling" indicates that this was characteristic of Sarah's behavior. Appealing to his women readers, Peter continues by affirming that they are the daughters of Sarah, her spiritual progeny. This is their state if they continue to do well and are "not afraid with any amazement." This apparently puzzling statement is another exhortation for women to trust themselves completely to God. The admonition throws light on the gentle and quiet spirit motif of verse 4. Rather than implying weakness, this spirit of quiet confidence enables the godly woman to avoid panic in the most desperate of circumstances. The word "amazement" is *ptoēsis* and refers to a state of terror or of being startled. Originally, it meant "fluttering," "perturbation of spirit," or "vehement emotion."[3] Saintly women are composed women who do not fear the terror-inducing incident.

---

[3]Liddell and Scott, *Greek-English Lexicon*, p. 1548.

Expressions Women Honor (3:7)

7—Likewise, ye husbands, dwell with them according to knowledge, giving honor unto the wife, as unto the weaker vessel, and as being heirs together of the grace of life; that your prayers be not hindered.

Verse 7. The elegance God honors together with examples men honor, have comprised the content of the first six verses. The last verse of this section on domestic relationships examines expressions women honor. The verse is devoted to an analysis of the role of the husband. Some might object that Peter is unfair to write more than three times as much about women as he did about men. But quality is the consideration here and not simply quantity. What is said to men in verse 7 is a weighty charge equal to, if not exceeding, the stringency of the assignment given to women.

There are two assignments coupled with two reasons for such action. First, husbands are to dwell with wives according to knowledge. Literally the phrase is *sunoikountes*, which couples the word *oikos*, or "house," with *sun*, the preposition meaning "together." Husbands are homemakers, too! They are to make the home *together* with their wives. This is to be accomplished according to "knowledge." (The precise nature of this knowledge is not provided. Bigg assumes that "the Pauline sense of *gnōsis*["knowledge"], in which it signifies the understanding of spiritual mysteries, is quite foreign to St. Peter."[4] But even if Bigg is correct in his insistence that the "knowledge" in view is only a general sensitivity and sensibleness, those attributes are only enhanced by the light cast upon them by the greater *gnōsis*, that is, comprehension of spiritual truths. Besides, *gnōsis* is another one of those words that the Christian community had appropriated for its own use, as can be seen in Paul's writings.)

---

[4]Bigg, *Commentary on St. Peter and St. Jude*, p. 154.

Two things are in view. First, husbands need a thorough understanding of the purpose and will of God. Relative biblical ignorance never reduces domestic problems. Second, profound insight into one's own wife—her attitudes, desires, and needs—is a concomitant. The possession of this knowledge will prepare the husband's heart for the second demand.

The second mandate is that of bestowing honor on the weaker vessel. "Vessel" is *skeuos*, which means anything from a household utensil to a piece of furniture. The wife is described as the "weaker vessel," a reference only to the biological endowments of the sexes, not to intellect or even durability. The husband is admonished to give honor to the wife. "Honor" is *timē*, a word used to describe something which is a great treasure, such as a precious stone. Such treasures are accorded the ultimate in care and protection. Furthermore, honor is paid to such treasures. This same attitude is to prevail among husbands in relation to their wives.

Two reasons are given for insistence upon these actions. To begin with, this behavior is expected since the two together are heirs "of the grace of life." Henry Alford is persuaded that Peter means "eternal life."[5] Perhaps so, but the very same statement could be handily affirmed concerning life in the present era. Too frequently Christians have failed to see that the grace of God is at work in creation as well as in redemption. As Samuel Mikolaski said in his superb analysis of grace, "Primary to both creation and redemption is grace."[6] That there is a cosmos, that we have life, that we have a capacity to know and to experience God—all of that is the product of God's grace. So, too, is the reality of the profound human relationships that bind us together in the home—a product of God's favor. Peter's argument is that since both husband and wife have inherited, not earned, temporal existence and eter-

---

[5]Henry Alford, *The Greek Testament with a Critically Revised Text,* vol. IV, p. 359.
[6]Samuel J. Mikolaski, *The Grace of God,* p. 16.

nal life, the husband should treat the wife with *timē*, knowing that she is an heiress of God's grace.

The second rationale for such behavior is the success or failure of the spiritual life of the husband. "Hindered" is translated *enkoptō*. *Koptō* literally means "to strike" or even "to cut off." The husband faces a possible interruption of his own devotional walk with God if he fails to live with his wife knowledgeably, giving due honor to her. His prayers may be "cut off," "chopped down!" The gravity which the apostle attaches to the duties of the husband in verse 7 begins to emerge in the light of this warning. Why would God assess such a consequence to a man's failure to respond properly to his wife?

The answer is found in God's use of the home as the chief metaphor and, therefore, the principal vehicle of instruction for teaching the appropriate relationships between man and God. For example, in the Old Testament, Israel is the wife of Jehovah. In the New Testament the church is the bride of Christ, the Bridegroom. The redeemed are the children of God via adoption and become brothers and sisters in Christ. Even salvation is cast in a family mold when it is described as a "new birth." Furthermore, the home is the basic unity of society. Failure in the homes of society will practically ensure the decadency of the social order.

The idea of the verse is not that a man cannot approach God until he is at peace with his wife. On the other hand, the verse poignantly suggests that a man's failure to be faithful to God's express commands for care of the wife can result in the interruption of his devotional walk with God.

To Love Life

1. Common Courtesies (3:8-9)
2. Consequent Characteristics (3:10-12)
3. Confident Counsels (3:13-17)

Author's Translation (3:8-17)

8—And in conclusion [let] all be of the same mind, compassionate, loving the brethren, tender-hearted, humble-minded,

9—Not returning evil against evil or insult against insult, but to the contrary speaking praise, because unto this [way of life] you were called in order that you might inherit praise.

10—For the one desiring to love life, and to see good days, let him restrain the tongue from evil, the lips not uttering deceit.

11—Let him turn away from evil and let him do good. Let him seek peace and let him follow it eagerly.

12—Because the eyes of the Lord are upon the righteous and His ears [are open] to their supplication, but the face of the Lord is against the ones doing evil.

13—And who is the one causing you evil if you should become zealous for good?

14—But even if you should suffer because of righteousness, you are blessed. And do not be afraid of their terror neither be disquieted.

15—But sanctify the Lord [as] Christ in your hearts, ready always for an apology to everyone who is asking you a word concerning the hope in you.

16—But with gentleness and reverence, having a good conscience so that in that which you are accused the ones who are insulting your good conduct in Christ may be put to shame.

17—For it is better, if the will of God should dictate, [to suffer] while doing good than to suffer while doing evil.

Common Courtesies (3:8-9)

8—Finally, be ye all of one mind, having compassion one of another, love as brethren, be pitiful, be courteous:

9—Not rendering evil for evil, or railing for railing: but contrariwise blessing; knowing that ye are thereunto called, that ye should inherit a blessing.

Having discussed the pivotal relationship which exists between husbands and wives, Peter advances to a more general discussion in which he provides a general outline for the programming of a significant life. To love life and to see good days is the theme of the section. In turn, the passage may be further divided into discussions of common courtesies (vv. 8-9), consequent characteristics (vv. 10-12), and confident counsels (vv. 13-17).

Verse 8. "Finally" does not suggest a premature conclusion to the book. However, it does signal a logical rehearsal of general spiritual attitudes following the more specific elucidation of domestic regulations. The phrase "of one mind" is *homophrones*, combining the words *homo* or "same" and *phrones*, "mind." As indicated earlier, *phrones* derives from *phrēn* which originally meant "diaphragm." In fact, one can see the Greek word within the English equivalent. According to Bertram, the diaphragm was regarded by the ancients as the seat of intellectual and spiritual activity.[1]

Such a perception may at first seem primitive. More careful reflection will tend to exonerate ancient man from charges of gross ignorance. Consider what happens to the brain, for example, when it becomes oxygen starved. Recall the vivid portrayal of creation in Genesis 1 and 2, in which man is

---

[1]Kittel, *Theological Dictionary*, vol. IX, p. 220.

created physically whole though still in need of God's act of "breathing into his nostrils the breath of life." Only then does the physical body become a thinking, feeling, volitional entity. A sort of reenactment of the same scene on a broader scale occurs in Ezekiel 37 in the "valley of dry bones" vision. After the bodies, certainly including the cranial contents, are whole, Ezekiel must still "prophesy to the wind" to blow upon the slain. Only then do they stand.

The ancients recognized that somehow the presence or absence of a pivotal aspect of spiritual life was associated with the ability of the body to breathe. To be cognitive, one had to have more than just a multicellular brain, he must possess breath. This probably accounts for the strange phenomena in both Hebrew and Greek in which the word for "wind" or "breath" is also the word for "spirit." In Hebrew *ru'ah* may mean any of the three while the Greek word *pneuma* has those same potentialities. In other words, the biblical writers knew that life was more than just a bodily phenomenon. Thus, the diaphragm gradually became identified with the capacity to know and to think.

The request of Peter is that believers be of the same mind. He does not intend that men become mental clones of one another. That would stifle creativity. He does mean that Christians are to be of the same mind regarding spiritual attitudes and godly actions. Furthermore, the saints are to be "compassionate." The term thus translated is *sumpathēs*, which provides the English lanugage with its word "sympathy." Literally, the idea involves the word "suffer" with the Greek preposition *sun*, which means "together." Christians should suffer with one another and "have compassion."

Sympathy would be possible without respect. Therefore, the additional command to "love as brethren" is given. The word is the well-known *philadelphos* combining *adelphos*, "brother," and *philos*, "love." Anyone who has listened to much preaching is aware of the various Greek terms for love—*agapē*, *philos*, and *eros*. If, however, there were ever a case of verbal pollution, one may find it in the frequently ill-informed discussions of these words. Yet, among the careful scholars there is general consensus. Trench says,

> For it should not be forgotten that *agapē* is a word born within the bosom of revealed religion. . . .[2]

This statement demonstrates the conclusion of most observers that the authors of the New Testament found *eros* totally foreign to what they meant by love. *Philos*, on the other hand, though acceptable in many contexts, still failed to capture all the import of the blossoming concept of love which ripened into full bloom in the incarnation and the atonement of Jesus.

Moulton and Milligan recognize that *philos* and *agapē* are considered virtually synonymous by many. However, they allow the distinction of the love of "friendship" for the former and "reverential love" for the latter.[3] Anders Nygren, in his major treatise on love, builds upon this distinction, citing four characteristics of *agapē*.

(1) *Agapē* is spontaneous and unmotivated.
(2) *Agapē* is indifferent to value.
(3) *Agapē* is creative.
(4) *Agapē* is the initiator of fellowship with God.[4]

Nygren's four characteristics distinguish clearly between the selfless *agapē*, and the selfish *eros*. Perhaps inadvertently, Nygren also posited the distinctions between *agapē* and *philos*. Both *agapē* and *philos* can be creative and, to a limited degree, can even provide grounds for relationships between God and man. But only *agapē* is unmotivated and indifferent to value. To return to the text of First Peter, the command to love as

---

[2]Richard C. Trench, *Synonyms of the New Testament*, p. 43.

[3]James Hope Moulton and George Milligan, *The Vocabulary of the Greek Testament*, p. 669.

[4]Anders Nygren, *Agape and Eros*, pp. 75-81.

brethren seems to be a mandate to sustain warm personal regard for the brethren rather than merely condescending to suffer with another simply because it is right.

The last two terms in the verse further define the interpersonal responses of holiness. Today "pitiful" means "pathetic" or even "sorry" in its censorious vein. Actually the Greek word *eusplanchnon* employs *splanchnon*, a word referring to the viscera or bowels with the prefix *eu* meaning "good." Gradually *splanchnon* came to incorporate in its sense all major internal organs and, hence, the heart—the seat of affection. Therefore, "good-hearted" or "tenderhearted" would capture the major thrust of the phrase.

"Courteous" translates *tapeinophrones*, combining the word for "mind" (see p. 49 in chap. 2) and *tapeinos*, which suggests "humble" or "lowly." The translation "humble-minded" seems preferable, although such a state would almost certainly produce a courteous approach requested in the King James Version translation.

Verse 9. In 2:23 Peter chronicled the response of Jesus to the assaults of the Romans and the Jews. Here he urges his readers to imitate this behavior in their own moments of persecution. If such crises have not already developed, it is clear that Peter anticipates them shortly. For both evils done and railings uttered, the Christian rejoinder is to be "blessing." "Blessing" is the King James Version translation of *eulogountes*, from which the English word "eulogy" derives. Literally it means a "good word." Proverbs 15:1 indicates that "a soft answer turneth away wrath." The necessity of returning good for evil is a matter of the calling of the Christian. The saint's calling is not only to be saved but also to act redemptively.

The reward for such deportment is the inheriting of a blessing. Once again "blessing" is *eulogia*. Perhaps this is the "well done, thou good and faithful servant" mentioned by Jesus. The fact that this commendation from God is promised in terms of an inheritance suggests that its realization may not be immediate. Although God's mercies are precious even now, a valuable concept for the believer is that of willingness to wait for his reward.

Consequent Characteristics (3:10-12)

10—For he that will love life, and see good days, let him refrain his tongue from evil, and his lips that they speak no guile:

11—Let him eschew evil, and do good; let him seek peace, and ensue it.

12—For the eyes of the Lord are over the righteous, and his ears are open unto their prayers: but the face of the Lord is against them that do evil.

Verse 10. Nevertheless, temporal and earthly blessings do accrue to the faithful servant of Christ. In part these are a natural consequence of certain approaches to life. These benefits are now cited by means of an appeal to a long quotation from Psalm 34:12-16. The psalm unfolds five proposals which, if followed, result in "having life" and "seeing good days."

(1) Refrain the tongue from evil.

(2) Let lips speak no guile.

(3) Eschew evil.

(4) Do good.

(5) Seek peace.

"Refrain" is a strong word, *pauō*, in the imperative mood. The translation "restrain" more adequately suggests the vigorous struggle which men face in order to avoid speaking evil. *Pauō* means anything from "hinder" or "give rest from a thing" to "stop or silence by death".[5] Peter's advocacy for such vigorous suppression of the tongue is supported by the lengthy discussion of James 3:1-12 in which the Lord's half-brother suggests that it is easier to tame carnivorous beasts, to steer great ships, or to douse flames than it is to harness the tongue. He calls the tongue a world of iniquity, a fire, an unruly evil which is full of deadly poison, and a little member that boasteth great things. These delineations specify the possibilities bound up in Peter's one word *kakos,* "evil." The basic misuses of speech are these:

(1) Boastfulness (see James 3:5)

(2) Iniquity (see James 3:6)

(3) Misrepresentation (see James 3:8-9)

Boastfulness and iniquity are covered by Peter's word *kakos.* Misrepresentation is the subject of the last phrase of the verse: "and his lips that they speak no guile" (v. 10). In turn, these two basic categories correspond to the two commands of verse 9, not rendering evil for evil or railing for railing.

Verse 11. The third general instruction to those who wish to love life and see good is to "eschew evil." "Evil" is still the word *kakos,* as in the previous verse. Whereas the former verse alluded to evil speech, the present verse prohibits evil activities. "Eschew" is *ekklinatō,* which comes from *klinō,* "to bend" or "to slope," from which comes the English word "clinic." It may also mean "to lay down" and in a slightly altered form may refer to a small bed or couch. Here the *ek* prefixing the word means "out." The believer is instructed "to bend his way out of" the path of evil.

Positively, he is to do good. Here once again Peter's frequent contrast between *kakos* and *agathos* is center stage. Further, the believer is to "seek peace, and ensue it." The two terms "seek" and "ensue" are vigorous Greek terms *zēteō* and *diōkō.* The word *zēteō* means "seek diligently." *Diōkō* is an even more energetic term meaning "to press forward," "to follow eagerly," and sometimes it is rendered "to persecute," as in Matthew 5:10. When it is thus translated, it really means "to pursue with malignity." Peace is not to be accepted or even merely promoted. Peace is to be avidly pursued.

Verse 12. The rationale which Peter presents for this kind of behavior involves the doctrines of God's omniscience, providence, and justice. First, Simon reminds his readers that the eyes of the Lord are upon the righteous. He is not oblivious to

---

[5]Liddell and Scott, *Greek-English Lexicon,* p. 1350.

their circumstances nor is he uninformed about the injustices which they might experience. Furthermore, God's ears are always open to the supplication of His children. Several crucial insights are resident in these two assertions. First, this is clearly anthropomorphic language. God is spirit, but the psalmist, who is cited by Peter, attributes to God certain physical attributes designed to communicate to readers the ability of God to intervene in behalf of His followers.

Three things are stressed: (1) God knows, (2) God hears, and (3) God sets His face against the wicked. If a disciple knows that his master knows about the trial, hears his requests, and will oppose those who abuse him, then he has all the impetus necessary to return good for evil and a pleasant word for insult. In Romans 12:19, Paul urges the same posture. Paul's readers are not to avenge themselves because God has declared that vengeance belongs to Him and that He will repay.

And interesting contrast in verse 12 juxtaposes two phrases.

The eyes of the Lord are over (*epi*) the righteous. . .
But the face of the Lord is against (*epi*) them that do evil.

Note that the same preposition, *epi*, is translated "over" and "against." Observe also the obvious contrast between "eyes" and "face." The prepositions are different from one another in the Hebrew of the psalm. But the real contrast is between "face" and "eyes." A reference to the "eyes" of God is simply a way of stressing that God sees all; He is omniscient. But the "face" of God is always a matter of awe and fear in the Old Testament. In Exodus 33:20 God tells Moses that he cannot see God's face and live. In Genesis 32:30 Jacob renamed the place in which he wrestles with the angel *Peniel*, "the face of God," because he said, "I have seen God face to face and my life is preserved."

God views with all-knowing compassion the sufferings of

the righteous and is instantly attentive to their cries. But He sets His face like flint against those who do wickedly. Their experience of God is only that of His stern displeasure.

Confident Counsels (3:13-17)

13—And who is he that will harm you, if ye be followers of that which is good?

14—But and if ye suffer for righteousness' sake, happy are ye: and be not afraid of their terror, neither be troubled;

15—But sanctify the Lord God in your hearts: and be ready always to give an answer to every man that asketh you a reason of the hope that is in you with meekness and fear:

16—Having a good conscience; that whereas they speak evil of you, as of evildoers, they may be ashamed that falsely accuse your good conversation in Christ.

17—For it is better, if the will of God be so, that ye suffer for well doing, than for evil doing.

Verse 13. The logical conclusion follows. Who will harm you if you are followers of that which is good? Of course, Peter's appeal is to ultimate harm. He knows well enough the potential for physical injury, death, and public humiliation. But from the pilgrim perspective already announced those human adversities are merely God's universities. Not only does the pilgrim learn trust, but he also has the opportunity to imitate Christ by loving and praying for his persecutors. He does this while resting in the knowledge that none of those things brings permanent harm. The word "harm" is *kakōsōn,* a verbal form of *kakos,* which Peter has already used repeatedly. The basic meaning of "evil" in an almost universally inclusive sense is intended. No one is able to perpetuate any ultimate evil upon the disciple who ardently practices good.

Verse 14. That the fisherman-missionary intends permanent rather than temporal harm is observable in the possibilities posited in this verse. "If you should suffer" is a translation of *paschoite,* a verb meaning "to suffer." The unusual feature of the verb is that it is in the optative mood, which is relatively rare in the Greek New Testament. The Greek language has one mood of reality and three moods of potentiality. The indicative mood is utilized when one speaks of something that is factual history, present happening, or future certainty. The imperative mood is the mood of command. The subjunctive mood is the mood of possibility, usually within a given context or circumstance. The optative mood is also a mood of possibility but usually without reference to existing conditions. It is the mood in which a wish or a desire is most often expressed.[6] For example, in this text no particular instance or threat of imminent persecution is in view. Peter knows, however, that such persecutions are possible, perhaps even inevitable. So, he employs the optative mood to say that if you should suffer for righteousness sake, you will be happy.

"Happy" is just one word in the plural form, *makarioi*. A very literal reading of the text would be, "but, if you should suffer for righteousness sake, happinesses!" The word represents an enviable state of blessedness. This state of happiness should be sufficient to prevent the Christian from fearing the terror of others. Both words, "terror" and "afraid," derive from the same word, "terror" (*phobos*) being a noun and "afraid" (*phobeomai*) being a verb. The idea is that in the event of persecution, the apostle's readers will not be forced to tremble before the forces that bring terror to most men because they are cognizant that the eyes of the Lord are upon the righteous. Neither will the Christian be troubled or disquieted.

Verse 15. In the midst of such potential upheavals, the follower of Christ should stand ready to seize the moment as an opportunity for witness. This begins by "sanctifying the Lord Christ" in one's heart. The expression is strange to our ears since we think of men rather than God needing sanctification. The word is *hagiasate*, an imperative verb, the root meaning of which is "distinction" or "separation." The idea

---

[6]H. E. Dana and Julius R. Mantey, *A Manual Grammar of the Greek New Testament*, p. 166.

here is that God is to be given a special place in the disciple's heart. The King James Version text reads "Lord God," but the overwhelming manuscript evidence favors "Lord Christ." Probably, Peter meant "set apart the Lord as the Anointed One of God [Christ] in your heart."[7]

Furthermore, the disciples are to be ready always to give an answer to those who inquire as to the nature of their hope. "Answer" is *apologia*, a word which comes into English as "apology." Originally it meant to provide a credible explanation for one's persuasion. That meaning is maintained in the Christian discipline of apologetics which is the marshalling of the evidences from all possible sources that indicate the veracity of claims to Christian truth. Such a request surely implies that the Christian faith is neither alogical nor illogical. Points within the faith are supralogical, that is, they transcend human reason; but they do, in fact, make sense!

Martin Luther feared that the sophists would misuse the text. Their tendency was to exalt reason and attempt to refute the reasoning of unbelievers on the basis of the natural light of Aristotle rather than with the word of God.[8] But this is certainly a distortion of the text and the context. The context is that of suffering. In the midst of that suffering, observers will note the remarkable optimism or hope of the Christian. The absence of this hope in the life of unbelieving observers will cause them to inquire about the reason for the believer's hope.

Consequently, it is the victorious life of the disciple which engenders the sincere query. "Reason" is *logos* which provides our English word "logic." The idea of the whole passage is thus clarified. Out of triumph in suffering, opportunities will present themselves for godly sufferers to give a defense of their position in Christ in terms of a logical statement of what God has accomplished in Christ. Most commentators favor

---

[7]Selwyn, *First Epistle of Saint Peter*, p. 193.

[8]Jaraslav Pelikan, ed., *Luther's Works*, vol. 30, "The Catholic Epistles," p. 107.

the inclusion for the next phrase "with meekness and fear" with verse 16. However, the logic of the choice of the King James Version translators is also appealing. The apology given should not be offered boastfully, but in meekness and with reverence for God.

Verse 16. The subject of accusation and response is now broached again, this time in the light of God's providence rather than, as before, in the light of Christ's example. Peter returns to the theme of Christ's example in 3:18. Here he speaks of putting to silence those who attack first by maintaining a good conscience. "Conscience" is *suneidēsis* which combines a word meaning "know" with the preposition *sun,* meaning "with." Conscience may be defined as a thinking mind illuminated by the revelation of God. The conscience can become "seared as with a hot iron" (1 Tim. 4:2), making it insensitive or even impervious to the light of God. But the word seems to indicate that capacity which the human mind alone has to know with the help of God's revelation the distinctions between right and wrong. A "good" conscience would be a sensitive, well-informed conscience.

The presence of this good conscience will enable the disciple through good conduct to put to shame those accusers guilty of insult. "Shame" is the emphatic *kataischunō,* which employs *aischunō,* meaning in itself "to be ashamed." *Kata,* the basic sense of which is "down" is attached making the term vividly express "shame down" or "disgrace." The expression "falsely accuse" is a rare word in the New Testament. It means to "calumniate" or "insult." It should be carefully noted that those who insult believers are to be shamed not by reciprocal attack but by impeccable conduct.

Verse 17. The final verse in this section seems only to state the obvious. It is preferred that the saints suffer unjustly while in the process of doing good than that they suffer justly for evil. The problem raised by the verse is the rather unusual expression involving the appearance of "will," *thelēma,* and "wish" or "desire," *theloi.* As can be readily observed, the two words derive from the same root. The two nearly identical words, one a verb, the other a noun, appearing so near one another in the same sentence pose something of a translation problem. But the theological problem is more severe.

In the Greek text, the sentence almost seems to suggest that God sanctions, wishes or desires that His servants might suffer. In questions of this nature the timeless distinction between the permissive and directive will of God must be involved. As in the case of Job, God may allow Satan to afflict His followers temporarily. Other testings unrelated to the work of the devil may also be allowable. However, two affirmations may be safely urged. First, God never enjoys or desires the suffering of even a sparrow. He notes even the fall of such insignificant creatures. Second, when His own followers endure temporary tribulation, the principle of Romans 8:28 surfaces. The verse assures us that a just God will teach us in the midst of the dilemma and reward us beyond the ravages of anything we must endure.

The Spirits in Prison

1. Propitiation for Sinners (3:18)
2. Proclamation to Spirits (3:19-20)
3. Profession of Saints (3:21-22)

Author's Translation (3:18-22)

18—Because Christ also died once concerning your sins, the just for the unjust, so that you might be conducted to God, having been put to death in the flesh but made alive by the spirit.

19—In which also he went and preached to the spirits in prison,

20—Who were once disobedient when the patience of God delayed in the days of Noah when the ark was being prepared, with the result that a few, that is, eight souls, were saved through water.

21—Which antitype, baptism, also now saves us, not the disposing of the pollution of the flesh, but the pledge of a good conscience unto God, through the resurrection of Jesus Christ.

22—Who is at the right hand of God, having entered into heaven, angels, authorities and powers having been subjected to him.

Propitiation For Sinners (3:18)

18—For Christ also hath once suffered for sins, the just for the unjust, that he might bring us to God, being put to death in the flesh, but quickened by the Spirit.

The passage to which we have now come is the most disputed passage in First Peter. Perhaps it even qualifies as one of the most difficult passages in the Bible. The enigmatic nature of the text itself is sufficient to force most interpreters to admit that certainty eludes the scholars. Unfortunately, many give only brief analysis and move on to less obscure texts. The serious student's task is made more perplexing by the fact that a number of the passages of similar challenge and equal dispute are potentially involved in the successful interpretation of this text. However, if dogmatic certainty is impossible regarding the full meaning of Peter's words, much can nonetheless be gleaned from the text by careful study. The approach will focus first on propitiation for sinners (v. 18), then proceed to an analysis of proclamation to prisoners (vv. 19-20), and finally culminate in the profession of saints (vv. 21-22).

Verse 18. For the third time in this brief epistle the substitutionary nature of the atonement is affirmed. Christ died "concerning your sins." It was a matter of the just "for the unjust," the design of which was to ferry men to God. The prepositions in the verse are pivotal in mastering the significance of Christ's death. Christ died "concerning" (*peri*) our sins. The preposition literally means "around" or in this case "with reference to." In other words, the death of Jesus did not occur with reference to an example, though surely His passion was exemplary. He died with reference to sin. The fact of human sin became the occasion for His passion.

Christ's death was also a case of the just "for" (*huper*) the unjust. The basic meaning of *huper* is "over." In order to grasp the full substitutionary character of the preposition as it is used here, a look at an identical use of the word in Galatians 3:10-13 will prove helpful. Three prepositions are employed by Paul in the Galatian passage. He declares all men to be "under" (*hupo*) the curse (v. 10). However, Christ through His death, redeemed us "from" (*ek*) the curse by being made a curse "for" (*huper*) us (v. 13). Since men are under the curse justly, they are freed from the curse by the substitutionary act of Christ in being made a curse (though He was just) for, or in the place of, us.

That is the same sense in which *huper* is applied in this text of First Peter. The clear intent of the preposition is enhanced by the nouns juxtaposed. The just died in behalf of the unjust. Such a concept has always seemed inconceivable to men who are uncomfortable with such ideas as God's wrath, the curse, or eternal punishment. Only two centuries after Christ, Plotinus, the father of Neoplatonic philosophy, said in the *Enneads*,

> For men who have become evil to demand that others should be their saviors by sacrifice of themselves is not lawful even in prayer.[1]

One may wish to follow Plotinus in rejecting the efficacy of Christ's death, but he should be fair with language. If he rejects the efficacy of the blood of Christ, then let him admit that he does so for philosophical reasons, not textual or hermeneutical considerations. Everywhere the subject is discussed, the Bible lucidly declares the vicarious nature of the death of Christ. Our "unjust" state called for the atonement. Christ's "just" nature made it possible for Him to provide it.

The effect of the death of Jesus was to bring men to God. Before the sacrifice of Jesus the way to God was barred by His holiness and justice and by our alienation and inadequacy. In His cross Jesus accepted the burden of our guilt (Is. 53:6) while transferring to us His righteousness (2 Cor. 5:21). This opened the way for men to be brought to God. The mood of the verb is subjunctive in sharp contrast to the indicative verb employed in the phrase "Christ died for your sins." This verb is indicative because the death of Christ as a propitiatory sacrifice is a fact of history, a reality. "That you might be brought to Christ" is subjunctive or potential because men

---

[1]Cited and translated by Bigg, *Commentary on St. Peter and St. Jude*, p. 160.

must choose to avail themselves of the way to God opened by Jesus.

The word translated "brought to God" (*prosagagō*) is also significant because it normally reflects an actual physical movement. However, the verb clearly means a spiritual journey in this context. The importance of that observation will become apparent in the discussion of the next verse.

Attention also needs to be focused on the sufficiency of our Lord's atoning sacrifice. The passage stresses that Christ died "once" (*hapax*) for our sins. No repeat is necessary. The adequacy of the Savior's sacrifice is such that His one sacrifice provides atonement for all who receive it.

The above is all reasonably clear in verse 18. The trouble begins in the exegesis of the last phrase of the verse, and its interpretation grows increasingly difficult as explanation of the next three verses is attempted. The final phrase declares that Christ was put to death in the flesh, an obvious reference to His physical demise on the cross by about three o'clock Friday afternoon. The remaining words can be translated "but made alive *in* the spirit" or "but made alive *by* the spirit." If the word in question (*pneumati*) is translated "in the spirit," then it is a dative of reference in Greek, meaning that Christ was made alive "with reference to" the spirit. The idea then is that when Jesus died in the flesh, His spirit was given life, and, in the spirit, He went to the underworld for some sort of preaching assignment.

In favor of this view is the grammatical construction. Undoubtedly, the phrase "put to death in the flesh (*sarki*) is a dative of reference. It means that Christ was put to death "with reference to" His flesh. The *men–de* particles, which mean essentially "on the one hand" and "on the other hand," provide still further evidence that the construction is absolutely parallel and that both *sarki* and *pneumati* are datives of reference.

If, on the other hand, *pneumati* is instrumental, then one would translate "made alive by the spirit." This would mean that the last phrase is not a reference to any event which took place immediately upon the expiration of Jesus. Instead, it would be a reference to the resurrection which occurred three days later. As Robert Leighton poignantly said, "He was indeed too great a morsel for the grave to digest."[2] He was put to death in the flesh, but God's Spirit raised Him from the dead on the third day. Selwyn insists that this is grammatically impossible.[3] Like others, Selwyn overlooks three critical considerations. (1) *Pneumati* can grammatically be instrumental just as well as it can be a dative of reference. (2) Actually the *men–de* construction, by its very nature, is designed to present two items which are antithetical to one another. The two items in this case are the death of Christ in the flesh and His dramatic resurrection by the power of the Spirit. (3) Even though grammar is important, it is always a mistake to insist that the writers of Scripture slavishly conform to what someone has enthroned as "normal" usage.

The ultimate question is not how did Peter say it, but what did Peter say? Those three considerations will go a long way at this point toward establishing a rather logical reading of the text as being essentially a presentation of the two pivotal aspects of Christ's work—His atonement and His resurrection.

Actually, there are numerous places in the New Testament where *pneumati* should be translated "by the spirit." Most of these make use of the preposition *en*, but not all of them. Consider Romans 8:14, "As many as are led by the Spirit [*pneumati*], they are the sons of God." Here you have the identical form *pneumati* clearly meaning "by means of." Other possible examples would be First Corinthians 14:2, Acts 18:5, Acts 20:22, and Luke 1:80. Admittedly some of those references can yield other meanings. But the instrumental working of the Holy Spirit is certainly plausible in those texts just as here.

Furthermore, what kind of sense does it make to say that at

---

[2]Robert Leighton, *Commentary on First Peter*, p. 352.
[3]Selwyn, *First Epistle of Saint Peter*, p. 196.

the time of Jesus' death His spirit was made alive? The spirit of Christ did not have to be made alive. The spirit of the Lord never died! His own last words from the cross were, "Father, into thy hands I commend my spirit." Some have imagined that this phrase has reference to the fact that Christ's spirit was somehow "set at liberty," or "no longer straightened." To say the very least, this would be the strangest possible use of the word translated "make alive." No evidence can be deduced to favor such views. Clearly the text is a contrast between the death of the body of Christ and His subsequent resurrection.

Proclamation to Spirits (3:19-20)

19—By which also he went and preached unto the spirits in prison;
20—Which sometime were disobedient, when once the longsuffering of God waited in the days of Noah, while the ark was a preparing, wherein few, that is, eight souls were saved by water.

Verse 19. Such a proliferation of views exists concerning these next two verses that over forty variations can be catalogued since the apostolic era. Luther said, "This is a strange text and certainly a more obscure passage than any other passage in the New Testament. I still do not know for sure what the apostle means."[4] For practical considerations all of these views can be effectively reduced to five major perspectives regarding its interpretation.

(1) Between the death of Jesus and His resurrection, Jesus descended into either *sheol* or *tartarus* to preach the gospel either to fallen angels or to lost antediluvians with a view to offering a second opportunity for salvation.

(2) In the interim between crucifixion and resurrection Christ descended into *sheol (decensus ad inferos)* to announce judgment upon the antediluvians.

(3) A descent took place at the same time proposed by the

---

[4]Pelikan, *Luther's Works*, vol. 30, "The Catholic Epistles," p. 113.

first two views, but the purpose was to announce judgment upon fallen angels. The place was *tartarus*, the prison for fallen angels (see 2 Peter 2:4).

(4) A descent took place in the same time period outlined above. However, Jesus went to paradise, the upper story of *sheol*, where Old Testament saints awaited the blood of Christ. Christ descended in order to lead these Old Testament saints to heaven.

(5) There was no *decensus ad inferos* at all. The reference is to Christ's preaching by means of the Spirit through Noah to the antediluvians.

The *first view* which supposes a *decensus* for the purpose of renewing opportunity for repentance finds support only among Roman Catholic theologians, liberal thinkers who wish to maintain a veneer of biblical theology while still maintaining universalist persuasions, and an occasional surprising Protestant, evangelical voice such as J. H. Jowett. The latter argues that, "No man's destiny is to be fixed until he has heard of Christ."[5] But this view is the very antithesis of the whole biblical witness and is unworthy of serious consideration. Paul declared in Romans 1:19-21 that God is manifest in all men, clearly comprehended, so that all men are without excuse. Knowing what men knew, they were ungrateful and refused to glorify God. The author of Hebrews adds, "And as it is appointed unto men once to die, but after this the judgment" (Heb. 9:27). In other words, judgment follows death, the latter having terminated opportunity for repentance.

The *second view* maintains that Christ descended into *hades*, a temporary prison for those who will be ultimately judged at the Great White Throne (see Rev. 20:11-15). The purpose of this *decensus* was to proclaim judgment upon the ungodly. Some who recognize the difficulty posed in this view by the mention of "Noah's day" urge that the preaching of Christ was only to the antediluvians. But the verb "preach" is *kērussō*,

---

[5] J. H. Jowett, *The Epistles of St. Peter*, p. 144.

which generally means "to preach the gospel" in the New Testament. Furthermore, it is difficult to imagine what purpose is served by announcing to men who are already suffering the pangs of *hades* (see Luke 16:22-23 where the English "hell" could better be translated "hades") that they are condemned or even that Christ has conquered. Surely both truths are already self-evident. Finally, if First Peter 4:6, which speaks of the gospel being preached (*euēngelisthē*) to the dead, treats the same matter, then the concept of judgment is ruled out entirely. Besides, the antediluvians are singled out, without apparent reason, when surely all the wicked dead should be included.

The *third view* reiterates the same scenario as the one dramatized in view two, except that the place of the descent and the objects of the preaching are changed. Christ's *decensus* is into *tartarus*, a prison where fallen angels are incarcerated until the final judgment. These "spirits" are the ones to whom Christ proclaims the victory of the cross. An important variation of this view involves the famous, vigorously disputed passage in Genesis 6:1-8. That text declares that the sons of God saw the daughters of men and cohabited with them. According to some, the progeny of those unions was a race of giants, or the *nephilim*. Furthermore, the "sons of God" is a reference to fallen angels who through coital union spawned a hybrid race of giants who were half human, half fallen angel.

The result of this demonic activity was that God found it necessary to destroy the earth, saving only Noah and his family. Since the time of the flood, those evil spirits which had resulted from the unions of earthly women and fallen angels have been confined to *tartarus* (2 Peter 2:4 and Jude 6). The *decensus ad inferos* of Jesus, between the time of His death and His resurrection, was to announce to these spirits in the prison of *tartarus* the triumph of Christ over Satan.

The problems with both variations are legion. First, surely such judgment or triumph must already be evident by virtue of their very confinement in chains (2 Peter 2:4). What then is the purpose of such proclamation? Besides, as indicated above, *kērussō* usually indicated the preaching of the doctrine of redemption. This again is especially the case if First Peter 4:6 is a connected reference.

However, the most questionable aspect of the whole approach is the practice of interpreting an obscure text on the basis of a tenuous interpretation of another equally enigmatic passage. The sons of God passage in Genesis is stretched considerably by the interpretation that the reference is to fallen angels and a hybrid race. The argument rests on three highly questionable assumptions.

(1) "Sons of God" (Gen. 6:2) must always refer to angels.

(2) "Giants" or "nephilim" (Gen. 6:4) is a reference to the hybrid race destroyed in the flood.

(3) "Men of renown" (Gen. 6:4) is a further reference to those same disobedient spirits.

A whole battery of facts militates against those conclusions. An excellent discussion that deals further with these difficulties may be found in J. Sidlow Baxter's *Studies in Problem Texts*.[6] Note the following difficulties.

(1) According to the author of Hebrews, angels are "spirits" and do not have or appropriate actual physical bodies (Heb. 1:7,14).

(2) Jesus declared that angels do not marry and, by implication, cannot marry (Matt. 22:30).

(3) Genesis 6:3 follows the mention of the "sons of God" with the declaration that, "My Spirit shall not always strive with *man*." Why is there no mention of fallen angels or demons as the cause for the coming flood?

(4) The emphasis of Genesis 6:2 is not on the "sons of God" but on the fact that they began choosing wives, multiple wives, thus creating polygamous relationships.

(5) "Sons of God" is an expression used only four other

---

[6]J. Sidlow Baxter, *Studies in Problem Texts*, pp. 146-192.

times in the entire Old Testament. Each time it is used of *good* angels, not of fallen angels, since it would be unthinkable to refer to fallen beings of any kind as "sons of God." In fact, the expression is clearly used in Job 1:6 and 2:1 as an expression of contrast to Satan, a fallen angel. Besides, how can a case be made that "sons of God" always means "angels" when only five total occurrences are available? After all, in Psalm 82:6 and John 10:34 men are even called *gods!* This is undoubtedly a very special use of the term, but it does verify that the context must be considered in the determination of meaning.

(6) If the flood was designed to destroy this hybrid race of *nephilim*, why do they appear again on the earth eight hundred years after the flood in Numbers 13:33? In fact, the *nephilim* are actually mentioned in Genesis 6:4 as apparently existing already when the "sons of God" came to the "daughters of men."

(7) If the *nephilim* were a hybrid race, half fallen angel and half human, could they have been redeemed? If not, as appears to be the case, a considerable problem emerges. Even the angels "who kept not their first estate" had a choice prior to their fall. So do all members of the human family. Must the innocent progeny of the hideous union of fallen angels be condemned simply because they were born of this union? Where is justice?

(8) The theory that fallen angels cohabited with women owes its origin not to the Scriptures but to the pseudepigrapha. The Book of Enoch and other pseudepigraphic writings provide the background for the "fallen angel" theory. The absence of canonical authority for such a theory is damaging at best.[7]

---

[7]Perhaps this is the appropriate time to comment that the whole idea of a *decensus ad inferos* is of suspect origin. One of the most extensive treatises on the subject is J. A. MacCulloch's *The Harrowing of Hell*, published in 1930 by T. & T. Clark in Edinburgh. MacCulloch documents the idea of a *decensus* from the myth of Heracles' descent to bring the dog Cerberus from Hades to that of Gilgames of Babylon to the Paradise of Utnapishtim to learn the secret of ·

(9) No one is able to establish the real meaning of *nephilim*. However, recent scholarship indicates that the word may not derive from *nēpel*, meaning "miscarriage" and ultimately, as a result of the untimely birth, "superhuman monstrosities." Rather, the term probably derives from *pala*, meaning "wonderful," "separate," "distinguishable" or "discriminate."[8] Therefore, the significance of the term *nephilim* may be descriptive of neither malignancy nor size. In fact, it may suggest the presence of some unusually "godly" men who were spiritually "distinguished" from the majority.

(10) This conclusion may indeed find further support from the expression "men of renown" in Genesis 6:4. This is obviously a synonym for *nephilim*, which occurs earlier in the same verse. Literally, the expression is "men of the name" (*aneshe hoshem*). Does the word *hoshem* mean "renown," or is it possible that it should be literally translated. If the latter is the case, then the phrase "men of the name" may actually mean "men of the name of God" or "men who are called by God's name." Support for such an analysis may be garnered in Numbers 16:2. Korah enlisted two hundred and fifty "men of name" in his rebellion against Moses. The expression "men of name" is identical with the one in Genesis 6:4 except that the article "the" is absent. Once again "men of name" may mean "men of the divine name."[9] Regardless of the accuracy of this

---

immortality (p. 25). In the ninth century *Apocalypse of Mary*, the virgin is depicted with patriarchs and prophets urging the Lord to take pity on those she has seen in hell (p. 35). MacCulloch clearly establishes the pre-Christian, non-Jewish, pagan origin of the whole idea of a *decensus*. Unlike the flood stories of other cultures in which the actual event preceded both biblical and cultural accounts, these multiple pagan descent sagas appeared long before the crucifixion of Jesus. This casts considerable doubt upon the possibility of an origin of the concept in revealed religion.

[8]Milton C. Fisher, *Theological Wordbook of the Old Testament*, vol. 2, ed. R. Laird Harris, Gleason L. Archer, Jr., and Bruce K. Waltke, p. 587.

[9]For this insight I am indebted to Dr. Leo Eddleman of the Criswell Center for Biblical Studies.

hypothesis, the evident problems associated with the fallen angel theory of Genesis 6 are staggering.

The *fourth view* takes a different twist altogether. There is still a *decensus*, but the thesis in this view is that Jesus spent the three days between His death and resurrection effecting the escape of Old Testament saints from *sheol* or *hades*. Prior to the atonement, the saved of the Old Testament could not enter directly into heaven. Therefore, they were retained in paradise, an upper story of *hades*, waiting the actual atoning sacrifice of Jesus. Having accomplished this atonement, Christ descended into paradise and preached to these "spirits" who had not yet received glorified bodies and announced to them their rescue. Cited as support for this thesis are such passages as Ephesians 4:8-10, in which Christ is said to have descended into the lower part of the earth. From thence He led captivity captive.

But once again problems abound. In the final analysis this view faces more serious objections than the view of a *decensus* to preach to fallen angels. Note the following.

(1) Instead of specifying all the Old Testament saints, one particular group is singled out, namely, those who lived in the time of Noah.

(2) Further, these spirits are not saints at all but are characterized as "disobedient spirits."

(3) Paradise is mentioned only three times in the New Testament. In Luke 23:43 Jesus promised the malefactor beside Him, "Today you will be with me in paradise." In Revelation 2:7, John the apostle looked from Patmos into the paradise where he saw the tree of life. Again in Second Corinthians 12:2 and 4, Paul was caught up into paradise, which is described as "the third heaven." In every case nothing could be more certain than that paradise is synonymous with "heaven," God's unique dwelling place. "Paradise" is a Persian loan word describing a lovely garden. It is synonymous with heaven, contains the tree of life, and was the immediate destination of Jesus following His death.

(4) Further verification of the location of paradise is found in the last words of Christ on the cross, "Father, into thy hands I commend my spirit" (Luke 23:46). Could such language possibly indicate a *decensus*? If the Lord's spirit went to the Father and His body was buried in the tomb of Joseph of Arimathea, what part of Him descended into *hades*?

(5) Two men in the Old Testament narrative were taken to be with God. Both Enoch and Elijah were miraculously translated. Of Enoch it is stated, "God took him." Where were these men taken? Certainly, the text does not indicate that their dwelling was to be a prison.

(6) The recipients of the preaching are "spirits in prison." Yet "paradise" means the very opposite of "prison." This would be the most unusual possible use of language.

(7) In Jesus' story of the rich man and Lazarus, the rich man is clearly in *hades*. But Lazarus is separated from him by a great gulf. In addition, Lazarus is comforted, a felicitous condition hardly worthy of being described as being "in prison."

(8) Paul indicates that "to be absent from the body" is "to be present with the Lord" (2 Cor. 5:8). Some insist that this condition is a post-atonement possibility not enjoyed by the Old Testament saints. But no evidence exists for an actual transfer of "paradise" from *hades* to the presence of God.

It is possible to argue that Old Testament saints were confined to paradise awaiting full atonement. Ephesians 4:8-10 and some other minor supporting texts such as Acts 2:27 and 31 can be marshalled to support the view that Jesus emptied paradise at the time of His own resurrection or ascension. It is *not* possible to tie those references to the present text since "disobedient spirits" are the recipients of this ministry. Consequently, the *fourth view* must be jettisoned.

The *fifth view* maintains that the preaching of Christ was accomplished by Noah in the days just prior to the flood. The Spirit of Christ preached through Noah to "disobedient spirits" who, at the time of Peter's writing, were shut up in prison forever. This is the author's perspective. I have selected this approach because there are fewer objections, and those which do exist are more easily solved than the objectionable features bound up in other views. Dogmatism is not in order. Nineteen centuries of exegesis have left scholars and Bible students thoroughly divided over the text. All that is in order is to share a perspective.

Primarily there are five objections to this view.

(1) "He went" (*poreutheis*) seems to imply actual journey. What justification is there for "spiritualizing" the term?

(2) In a cursory reading of the text, this journey certainly appears to have been made at the time of Christ's death.

(3) The word "prison" yields itself better to the idea of a "place" than to a "state of being."

(4) If paradise and heaven are synonyms and if *hades* is only a "state," why utilize these terms in such confusing ways?

(5) The appearance of Old Testament saints at the time of Christ's resurrection (Matt. 27:53) would seem to suggest that Christ invaded the realm of the dead and released its saintly captives.

The best approach to these problems will be to answer them through a careful exegesis of the passage. Four questions must be answered in verse 19. (1) What is the antecedent of "which?" (2) Who are the spirits in prison? (3) What was preached to the spirits? (4) In what sense can it be said that Jesus "went" to this preaching assignment?

"By which" is a correct translation of *en hō*. The antecedent of *hō*, "which," is *pneumati* or Spirit in verse 18. After Christ's death in the flesh, He was raised up by the Spirit. By means of this same Spirit that raised Him from the grave, He also went and preached to the spirits in prison. Selwyn objects that *hō* cannot have *pneumati* as its antecedent. Since there is no example in the New Testament where the dative of reference serves as an antecedent to a pronoun, therefore, the reference must be to the whole process alluded to in verse 18.[10]

---

[10]Selwyn, *First Epistle of Saint Peter*, p. 197.

In the exegesis of verse 18, it has already been shown that *pneumati* is probably not a dative of reference but an instrumental and should thus be translated "made alive by the Spirit" and viewed as a statement of the Lord's triumphant resurrection. On the other hand, *ho* is the necessary case, gender, and number to have *pneumati* as its antecedent. The question is not, as Selwyn imagines, what is customary *koine* Greek usage. The question is: What did Peter mean? The suggestion that the whole process described in verse 18 is the antecedent is even less plausible than to posit a relatively unusual grammatical structure. Jesus did not preach to the spirits in prison during the whole process of verse 18. While He was suffering on the cross, He was in Jerusalem, not in *hades* or paradise. Furthermore, He was dying and not preaching![11] The sense of the phrase remains, "By which Spirit, the same one that made Him alive in the resurrection, He went and preached to the spirits in prison."

Who were the "spirits in prison?" Verse 20 leaves no doubt. They were the disobedient spirits who lived in the days of Noah. The objection that "spirits" is a word which always refers to special orders of created beings other than man is simply not viable. The author of Hebrews speaks of the "spirits of just men made perfect" (Heb. 12:23). Paul speaks of a disembodied state in Second Corinthians 5 when only the spirit of a man continues in life.

God does not destroy without warning. The iniquity of the world had reached such vast proportion that God, after warning the people through the preaching of Noah, proceeded with the great flood. The text uses the verb *kerussō* meaning "to proclaim." Noah is specifically called a preacher (*kērux*) of righteousness by Peter in Second Peter 2:5. The word "preacher" is a nominal form of the verb *kerussō*. Peter thus pictures Noah as more than just a boat builder. He actively preached "righteousness." Nothing could be more

---

[11]Other scholars differ with Selwyn decidedly. See *An Idiom Book of New Testament Greek* by C. F. D. Moule (London: Cambridge Univ. Press, 1975), pp. 131-132.

natural than that both texts cite Noah as the actual preacher.

The location of the spirits is identified as "prison." There are two possible meanings. Peter may have had in mind the bondage of sin. The idea has been on Peter's lips before, as recorded by Luke in Acts 8:23. Simon the sorcerer sought to purchase the power of the Holy Spirit. Peter replied, "Thou art in the gall of bitterness and in the bond of iniquity." Paul, too, speaks of the unredeemed state as a form of bondage (Titus 3:3). If this is what is intended, then Peter is suggesting that Christ preached through Noah to the antediluvian generation, a generation enslaved in the prison of its own sin.

A more likely interpretation would be a diachronic view, i.e., a view that links a distant event with the present text. The preaching of the Spirit of Christ through Noah took place in the antediluvian era. But Peter speaks of the hearers of that preaching as they were at the time of the writing of Peter's epistle. This would explain why he calls them "spirits," since they would still be in a disembodied state until the time of the resurrection of the unjust (Dan. 12:2; Acts 24:15). It also provides a more adequate assessment of "prison." "Prison" (*phulakē*) is probably a reference to *hades*, the prison in which the wicked dead are held awaiting the day of final judgment. The sense then becomes that the Spirit of Christ through Noah preached before the flood to the rebellious generation, the same ones who are now imprisoned in *hades* awaiting the final judgment. The message preached was a warning of impending doom due to the iniquity of that generation. Surely it also included an offer of grace to the penitent, thus making Noah a preacher of righteousness.

But the fourth question is the most difficult for advocates of the fifth view. The text says that Christ went (*poreuomai*) and preached to the spirits in prison. Doubtless *poreuomai* usually means an actual journey. To make it a spiritual journey is risky exegesis, especially for those who normally champion a literal method of exegesis. The answer is that a spiritual journey is no less a literal journey than is a physical journey. As a matter of fact, *poreuomai* is used exactly as *prosagō*, "that he might bring us to God," is used in the preceding verse. Normally *prosagō* would be employed of physically transporting something or someone. The *prosagagous* appeared before a monarch to introduce to him a guest. But in First Peter 3:18, the word is used of a spiritual introduction to God even though this introduction will ultimately culminate in actually being ushered into God's presence (1 Cor. 13:12). Just as "bring us to God" is in this case a spiritual, yet actual, journey, so also Christ "went" (*poreuomai*) to the spirits now in prison by the power of the Spirit in the days of Noah.

Furthermore, *poreuomai* itself is used several places in the New Testament for a "spiritual" journey. In Luke 1:6 Zechariah and Elisabeth are pictured as "walking" (*poreuomai*) in all the commandments. In Acts 14:16 the nations are said "to walk" (*poreuomai*) in their own ways. In fact, Peter uses the term in a similar vein in First Peter 4:3 and Second Peter 3:3. This will be sufficient to illustrate that the word *poreuomai* does not *necessarily* demand interpretation as an actual physical journey. Besides, advocates of a *decensus* are in reality suggesting a spiritual journey. A journey of the Spirit of Christ to a rendezvous in *hades* is not essentially different than a journey of the Spirit of Christ to the antediluvians.

Verse 20. The twentieth verse identifies, as we have already observed, the spirits to whom Jesus preached. They were the disobedient people who lived during the days when Noah was preparing the ark. The reason for the mention of these spirits now appears. The gist of the entire passage is an exhortation to patience in suffering due to the example of Christ. God the Father was also "longsuffering." The word translates *makrothumia* and means "a long time to anger." Double emphasis is present through the vivid word *apexedecheto*, translated "waited." God is pictured as patiently waiting, restraining the just expression of His righteous indignation while Noah prepared the ark and preached his message of righteousness.

The result of this preaching of Noah might appear unsuccessful by some modern standards. Only seven converts were saved along with Noah, the eighth. This brings us to the last problem in this particular verse. The eight were saved *di hudatos*. Should this be interpreted as instrumental and rendered "saved by means of water," or should it be viewed as a matter of location and translated "saved in the midst of water." Grammatically, either is possible. But logically only one will suffice. The water by itself did not save anyone. Indeed it almost drowned everyone. The waters of the flood represented the inundation of the wrath of God. Those on the ark, representing God's program of deliverance were saved in the midst of the waters of the flood.

Profession of Saints (3:21-22)

21—The like figure whereunto even baptism doth also now save us (not the putting away of the filth of the flesh, but the answer of a good conscience toward God,) by the resurrection of Jesus Christ:

22—Who is gone into heaven, and is on the right hand of God; angels and authorities and powers being made subject unto him.

Verse 21. If verse 21 is less troublesome than 19 and 20, it is only slightly less so. The problem here is the significance of Christian baptism. A first reading of the verse appears to suggest that baptism either saves men or at least contributes to their salvation. Thus the verse has been cited for generations as a proof text by the various advocates of baptismal regeneration. But the verse in no sense advocates any saving significance for baptism.

Baptism is called a figure (*antitupos*). The word means literally "type" or "antitype." When a key is struck on a typewriter, it leaves a letter, such as "z," on the page. No, actually the letter "z" is still on the metal or plastic element which struck the page. What is on the page is a type or antitype which corresponds almost identically to the "z" on the metal or plastic element. In the same fashion, baptism saves us. It is not salvation, but it is a figure, an antitype, a picture of that salvation. Baptism is the public demonstration in which one pictures the spiritual transformation that has already occurred.

Peter continues by explaining precisely what he intended. Baptism never cleanses the filth of the flesh. However, since Christ commanded it, baptism must be accepted as the answer of a good conscience toward God. That good or cleansed conscience has come about as a result of the resurrection of Jesus Christ from the dead. In other words, anyone who has been saved, receiving a good conscience toward God, will answer by submitting to baptism as Jesus mandated. While baptism does not save, it is unthinkable that one who has been saved would reject baptism. To do so is to reject the command of Christ.

Baptism stands in the same relation to salvation that the ark and the flood stood to Noah. Noah found grace in the eyes of the Lord. God's grace saved him. Therefore, God pictured that salvation by saving Noah physically in the midst of the flood. The grace of God also saves men today (Eph. 2:8-9; Titus 3:5). Christ was immersed in death, one death, yet arose triumphant over it. We picture that vicarious sacrifice by our own immersion in water.

Should any doubt linger about what Peter means, it may be permanently dispelled by his statement recorded by Luke in Acts 10:47. Cornelius, the Roman centurion, had just been saved. Peter asked, "Can any man refuse water that these should not be baptized, which have received the Holy Ghost as well as we?" The argument is lucid. Even though Cornelius is a Gentile, he has received the Holy Spirit. No one can receive the Holy Spirit unless he has been saved (Rom. 8:11,14). Since Cornelius has been saved just as Peter had, can anyone legitimately deny to him the public witness of baptism? Baptism does not save. It is a figure of salvation to which obedience is the answer of a clear conscience toward God.

Verse 22. The mention of Christ's triumphant resurrection is the catalyst which launches Peter into a description of the subsequent phases of Christ's victory. Having suffered, He is now exalted, sitting in the place of honor at the right hand of God. Christ entered into heaven in His resurrected or glorified body at His ascension. He was no longer "spirit" alone. Mary Magdalene was clinging to real substance in the garden (John 20:17). Thomas was invited to feel the scars of real wounds (John 20:25,27), and Jesus Himself ate fish and a honeycomb (Luke 24:42). Yet Jesus was able to appear or disappear at will, walking through closed doors (John 20:19).

In this glorified and exalted state, all of the orders of heavenly spirits are subjugated to Him. Angels, authorities, and powers are mentioned. Possibly, the reference to "angels" is to unfallen spirits, while "authorities" and "powers" may refer to the orders of fallen angels who participated in the rebellion of Satan. This is unquestionably the meaning of one of the terms in Ephesians 6:12 where Paul says we wrestle against "powers" in our spiritual warfare. Christ, through His resurrection and ascension, has triumphed over all such foes as He is again exalted at the Father's right hand. (See charts on First Peter 3:18-22 in the Appendix.)

Preaching to the Dead

1. Sufficient Revellings (4:1-3)
2. Strange Righteousness (4:4-6)
3. Sagacious Reciprocity (4:7-11)

Author's Translation (4:1-11)

1—Therefore, since Christ suffered in the flesh, arm yourselves also with the same purpose because the one who has suffered in the flesh has ceased from sin,

2—that he should live no longer in the lusts of men but in the will of God during the time which remains in the flesh.

3—For the time having passed is sufficient to have practiced the counsel of the nations, having pursued outrageous behavior, lusts, drunkenness, lascivious feasting, drinking parties, and criminal idolatries.

4—In which they are astonished that you are not running into the same excess of profligacy, treating you contemptuously.

5—They shall give an account to the one who is ready to judge the living and the dead.

6—For unto this end the gospel was preached also to the dead so that they might be judged with regard to men in the flesh but made alive with regard to the Spirit of God.

7—But the end of all things has begun to draw near. Therefore, be sober-minded and determined in prayer.

8—Before all else having fervent love for one another, because love covers a multitude of sins.

9—[Be] Hospitable to one another without complaint;

10—As each has received a spiritual gift, using it to minister to one another as good stewards of the diverse grace of God.

11—If anyone is speaking, [let it be] as the oracle of God; if anyone is serving, [let it be done] as out of the strength which God supplies; so that in all things God may be glorified through Jesus Christ to whom is the glory and dominion unto the ages of the ages; amen!

Sufficient Revellings (4:1-3)

1—Forasmuch then as Christ hath suffered for us in the flesh, arm yourselves likewise with the same mind: for he that hath suffered in the flesh hath ceased from sin;

2—That he no longer should live the rest of his time in the flesh to the lusts of men, but to the will of God.

3—For the time past of our life may suffice us to have wrought the will of the Gentiles, when we walked in lasciviousness, lusts, excess of wine, revellings, banquetings, and abominable idolatries.

The apostle turns his attention to the ethical implications of Christian commitment and to the useful employment of spiritual gifts. The discussion begins with an assessment of the sufficiency of past revellings (vv. 1-3), proceeds to an elaboration of the strange righteousness which defies understanding among the nations (vv. 4-6), and terminates with an examination of the sagacious reciprocity involved in the use of spiritual gifts (vv. 7-11).

Verse 1. The sufferings of Christ again serve as the example and motivating impetus to the disciple to arm himself. But the panoply of the saints is neither sword and shield nor verbal stiletto. Rather, the believer is to be armed with the mind of Christ. The challenge recalls the words of Paul in Philippians 2, "Let this mind be in you, which was also in Christ Jesus" (v. 5). Specifically, if the Christian has the same mind as Christ with regard to suffering in th flesh, he will not be as vulnerable to the practices of the nations around him.

The difficulty in the verse concerns the function of the phrase, "He that has suffered in the flesh hath ceased from sin." Obviously, when a follower of Christ dies, he is finally free from sin. But while Christ's sufferings included His death, this does not appear to be the application which the apostle is making. The sense seems to be that those who have remained faithful to Christ even when that entailed suffering have proven themselves. The declaration that these have ceased from sin suggests not sinless perfection but rather an escape from the dominion and slavery of sin. "Ceased" is a translation of *pauō* which means "to rest." One who is willing to endure suffering as a part of his faith has rest from the domination of sin in his life.

Verse 2. That Peter did not intend physical death by his above avowal becomes evident in verse 2. A man "ceases" or "rests" from sin in the sense that his desires are to be obedient to the will of God rather than living in the lustful fashion which characterizes the nations. The mention of the remainder of his time in the flesh focuses on three distinct aspects or epochs in the life of the believer. First, there is the life which is "no longer" an option. This points to a moment of specific conversion, the gateway to a life whose major concern is the will of God. However, the verse also indicates that the second stage is still in the flesh. Since it is the "rest of the time" in the flesh, a limited span of time, which will ultimately give way to the eternal blessedness promised by the Lord, is involved.

Verse 3. Simon Peter's argument for abandonment of the behavior patterns of the nations now moves to a temporal expression. Sufficient *(arketos)* time has elapsed already in which the will of the nations had predominated. Of course, it could be argued that any time spent this way is enough, even too much. But Peter is simply saying that a sufficient amount of time has been squandered so that no more waste can be afforded. The wasting of life is found in "going" or "walking" *(poreuomai)* in a series of actions which are characteristic of the unconverted nations. Note that *poreuomai* is the same word used to describe the journey of Christ to preach to the imprisoned spirits (3:19). Both places point to a spiritual walk.

Six activities are introduced which characterize the nations but from which the saints should flee.

(1) Lasciviousness *(aselgeia)* means "license." Lightfoot's comment is cogent. "A man may be *akathartos* and hide his sin; he does not become *aselgēs* until he shocks public decency."[1] Lightfoot goes on to specify that in classical Greek the word usually indicates insolence or violence. The idea of open debauchery is at the heart of the term. The word is actually plural in this text, indicating repeated acts of license.

(2) Lust *(epithumia)* means "to move upon." *Thuō* originally denoted a violent movement of air, water, the ground, animals, or man.[2] The *epi* appended increases the "surge" communicated in the concept. In pre-Socratic Greek the word had no particular moral content. The word is still used in this morally neutral sense in the New Testament. But most frequently, the concept is that of compelling, evil desire.

(3) Excesses of wine *(oinophlugia)* is a reference to "drunkenness." The word *oinos*, "wine," is combined with the verb *phluō*, which means "to bubble" or "to overflow." Hence the idea of drunkenness exists wherever there is uninterrupted flow of wine.

(4) Revellings *(kōmos)* means "wild feasting" or "carousing." The word was used to describe the victory celebrations after wars. The idea encompasses everything from merrymaking to orgies.

(5) Banquetings *(potos)* means "drinking-bouts." The chief difference between this word and *oinophlugia* seems to be the public nature of *potos*. Whereas the former word might represent a relatively private affair; the latter denotes a party planned for the imbibing of spirits.

(6) Abominable idolatries *(athemitos eidōlolatpia)* indicates "unlawful idolatries." *Themis* refers to a law which is established by custom. The alpha privitive makes it "unlawful."

---

[1]J. B. Lightfoot, *The Epistle of Saint Paul to the Galatians,* p. 210.
[2]Kittel, *Theological Dictionary,* vol. III, p. 167.

"Idolatries" refers to all objects which become the focus of ultimate concern for a man. Gentile Christians are hereby reminded of the exclusive nature of their faith in Christ.

These six activities above were characteristic of Roman society. They remain characteristic of most affluent societies in the twentieth century. Shocking public license, unbridled desires for pleasure, drunkenness, a love for carousing, drinking bouts, and the unlawful worship of objects other than God paint a pathetic canvas of Roman society and modernity as well. The disciple is to demonstrate the uniqueness of his faith by separating himself from all such indulgence.

Strange Righteousness (4:4-6)

4—Wherein they think it strange that ye run not with them to the same excess of riot, speaking evil of you;

5—Who shall give account to him that is ready to judge the quick and the dead.

6—For for this cause was the gospel preached also to them that are dead, that they might be judged according to men in the flesh, but live according to God in the spirit.

Verse 4. Two consequences are inevitable when the disciple withdraws from participation in such activities as those listed above. First, the rest of the world concludes that the behavior of Christians is odd. Second, in reaction the ungodly who do such things become harshly critical of those who do not hasten to involve themselves in such debauchery. "Think it strange" is a translation of a poignant word, *xenizō*, which means "to be staggered with surprise." The point of this surprise is that the believer does not run with them into the same "excesses," a word which literally signifies "a pouring out." "Riot" is *asōtia*, the same word used by Jesus to depict the life-style of the prodigal son who spent his inheritance in "riotous living." Basically, the word means "undisciplined." Because Christians do not rush to such unrestrained excess, others speak evil *(blasphēmeō)* of them.

[153]

Several factors probably account for this blasphemy of the saints. First, the fact of the "strangeness" of behavior makes the Christian fail to fit the mold. Second, those who live in unrestrained excess intuitively know that this is wrong. Those who do not run to the same evils constitute a visible and provoking rebuke. The blasphemy becomes a method of re-directing attention and hopefully escaping the judgment which is felt.

Verse 5. However, God has the last word in these matters. Peter has already advanced the inevitability of suffering un-justly. Now he reminds his readers that God keeps reliable books on such matters. Further, as a God of justice, He is committed to rectifying injustice eventually. So those who *blaspheme* Christians for their separationist lives will involun-tarily give an account *(logos)* to the one who stands in readi-ness (literally, "has readiness") to judge the quick and the dead. "Quick" is a unique King James translation of *zōntas*, a word which means "living." The verse simply affirms that God will judge both those who were alive in Christ and those who were dead in trespasses and sin even though those judgments take place at different times and places. The verse may also be construed as a promise that those living, as well as those who have died, will be judged by God.

Verse 6. The connection between verse 6 and the "spirits in prison" passage of the previous chapter has already been suggested. In turn, the present verse assumes some of the same difficulties encountered in the former passage. There are four basic approaches to interpreting the verse.

(1) The verse is referring to the previous passage and states that Christ preached to the living on earth and the wicked dead of Noah's time in *hades*.

(2) The verse refers to the *decensus;* but since the preaching of the gospel is specified, this must be an announcement of deliverance to the saints confined in *paradise*.

(3) No *decensus* is pictured in this verse any more than in the previous passage. If there is a connection between the two

passages at all, the preaching of the gospel was made to living men at the time of Noah. These same men have since died and, by the time Peter writes, are called "the dead."

(4) The reference is unconnected with the previous passage and refers to the preaching of the gospel to those who are "dead in trespasses and in sins" (Matt. 8:22; Eph. 2:1; Col. 2:13).

Note must be taken that two possibilities are virtually eliminated by the present passage. Since the verse specifies the preaching of the gospel, the purpose of the preaching could not have been the formal announcement of judgment to any group. Whereas *kērussō* in 3:19 simply means "to proclaim" and could possibly be construed as the preaching of judgment, *euāngelizomai* is used in 4:6 and can mean nothing other than the proclamation of a good message. Furthermore, any possibility of 4:6 referring to proclamation of judgment to fallen angels is farfetched. As we have seen, the preaching is the proclamation of the gospel; whereas the Bible declares that the fate of the fallen angels is already determined (2 Peter 2:4; Jude 6). In any case, fallen angels are nowhere called "the dead." This expression yields itself only to the physical death of men or to the condition of spiritual lifelessness prior to the quickening of the new birth.

If Hebrews 9:27 restricts men to a decision for or against God in this life only, then position one—the idea that there was a *decensus* in which Christ preached to the dead antediluvians—is impossible because plainly it is the gospel which was preached. This would be pointless since these pre-flood sinners are already condemned.

The second view is more plausible except for the fact that we have shown in the previous chapter the impossibility of the "spirits in prison" passage having any connection to Old Testament saints. Remember, Christ's preaching was to "disobedient" spirits. Only the third and fourth interpretations are ultimately workable.

View number three, that Christ preached through Noah

prior to the flood to men who are, by the time Peter writes, dead and confined in *hades,* is the most probable, especially if the passage is connected with the "spirits in prison" passage. Since this connection is very likely, the author leans toward this understanding.

"For this cause" may be better translated "unto this end." In other words, because of the certainty of approaching judgment promised in verse 5, the gospel, or good news, was presented to the rebellious antediluvians prior to the devastation of the flood. This was done in the hope that, while they would be judged with reference to human standards as men in the flesh, they might also be made alive with reference to the Spirit of God. Apparently only seven besides Noah were receptive to this offer of life.

Sagacious Reciprocity (4:7-11)

7—But the end of all things is at hand: be ye therefore sober, and watch unto prayer.

8—And above all things have fervent charity among yourselves: for charity shall cover the multitude of sins.

9—Use hospitality one to another without grudging.

10—As every man hath received the gift, even so minister the same one to another, as good stewards of the manifold grace of God.

11—If any man speak, let him speak as the oracles of God; if any man minister, let him do it as of the ability which God giveth: that God in all things may be glorified through Jesus Christ, to whom be praise and dominion for ever and ever. Amen.

Verse 7. Having discussed the past, Peter turns to the present—but with an eye to the immediate future. He declares that the end of all things is at hand. Surely he did not intend that his readers understand that within a matter of days the cataclysmic destruction of the natural order, which this same apostle foresaw (2 Peter. 3:12), would occur. But even if this is not what he meant, the text, and others like it, seem difficult to reconcile with nineteen hundred years of history.

The initial step toward understanding what Peter had in mind is to see the apparent antithesis of this verse in Second Peter 3:3-9. In this passage, the apostle notes that as time elongates, scoffers will question the possibility of Christ's return. But the Lord is not slack in His promise, just long-suffering, giving every opportunity for repentance. Since nothing intervenes but the patience of God, the day of the Lord comes as a thief in the night.

These observations aid in comprehending Peter's intention in 4:7. He means that no other major intervening events are planned by God. The sequence of divine history is this: incarnation of the eternal Son of God, atonement, resurrection, ascension, pentecost, the return of Christ, and the everlasting kingdom. Pentecost is behind. The consummation of all things is at hand in that no other redemptive event is planned by God. The coming of Christ for His church is next!

The words employed also demonstrate this idea. "End" is *telos*, which, according to Delling, means "achievement" or "completion."[3] The expression "at hand" translates the Greek perfect tense verb *ēngiken*. Preisher suggests that the primary significance of *engizō* is "to draw near."[4] The achievement or completion of the redemptive plan of God has drawn near. The termination of the natural order (2 Peter 3:12) and even the return of Christ (2 Peter 3:3-9) may not happen immediately, but with all other facets of God's redemptive program having been completed, the final achievement lingers nearer than ever.

Consequently, the readers are urged to exhibit sobriety and to be watchful unto prayer. The sobriety about which Peter speaks "connotes the cool head and balanced mind which is the opposite of all *mania* or undue excitement. . . ."[5] "Watch unto prayer" employs another word for "sobriety," namely,

---

[3]Kittel, *Theological Dictionary*, vol. VIII, p. 49.
[4]*Ibid.*, vol. II, p. 330.
[5]Selwyn, *First Epistle of Saint Peter*, p. 216.

nēphō. Bauernfeind captures the figurative sense of this word when he states that, "what is in view is the unequivocal and immediately self-evident antithesis of all kinds of mental fuzziness."[6] Translated into what the apostle means in this text, all elements of life which might stupefy the Christian, turning his life away from incessant communion with God, must be laid aside. This produces sobriety in a life of prayer.

Verse 8. Loving actions ought also to characterize believers. Before all other actions, fervent charity or love ought to be the possession of all followers of Christ. Note that love *(agapē)* is defined as not only an attitude but also a volitional act. This is because the nature of *agapē* is selfless, extended regardless of the worthiness of its object. "Fervent" is an injunction to love intensely and with determination.

The rationale for this love is that "love covers a multitude of sins." The sage of Proverbs 10:12 says, "Hatred stirreth up strifes: but love covereth all sins." The idea of a "covering" embodies terminology that is reminiscent of the language of Old Testament sacrifice. Love does not deny the fact of offenses, but it does cover them over rather than reveal them for judgment. Again, this is precisely the message of Christ's atonement. The blood of Christ, as the ultimate expression of love, covers a multitude *(plēthos)* of our sins. By the same token, the love of believers for one another would cover a multitude of sins within the community, not in the sense of atonement, but in the sense of hiding from harsh judgment.

Verse 9. "Be hospitable" is the translation of *philoxenoi*, which is a compound word made up of *philos*, "love," and *xenos*, "stranger." The word originally meant "to love strangers." Here it is actually a noun, depending on the verb "having" in the previous verse. While life in the Christian community should be characterized by those having fervent love, these same individuals should demonstrate that love by extending hospitality. Furthermore, this hospitality should be

---

[6]Kittel, *Theological Dictionary*, vol. IV, p. 937.

undertaken willingly, "without grudging." The word translated "grudging" might be better rendered "complaint." It is almost an onomatopoetic word. The Greek term is *gongusmos*, "murmuring."

Verse 10. The last two verses of this section of the epistle address the use of spiritual gifts. They strongly parallel the writing of Paul in First Corinthians 12—14, by insisting that the purpose of these gifts is to minister to the saints. Several insights to the nature and use of spiritual gifts may be readily gleaned from these verses.

(1) "Each person is to employ the gift which he has received." Clearly Peter believed that every member of the body of Christ possessed one or more such gifts.

(2) "Gifts" is *charisma*, literally "grace gift." The gift is undeserved and unsought, sovereignly provided by the will of God. Elsewhere, Paul also calls them *pneumatika*, "spirituals," indicating that these are gifts which operate in the spiritual realm, even though they may certainly have physical expression.

(3) The church is to "minister" these gifts to one another. "Minister" is a reading of *diakoneō*, the word which becomes the English word "deacon." The reference was originally to one who waits on tables. The servant idea is strong in the word, suggesting that spiritual gifts are definitely to be used in service to others and not to engender self-satisfaction or spiritual pride.

(4) "Stewards" is still another emphasis placed upon the servant nature of the gifts (see discussion of *oikonomos* in 2:18). The *oikonomos* or "steward" really has nothing of his own. He manages perhaps the entire estate of his master, but the riches at his disposal are not his own. His success is measured in terms of how well he manages these stores. The *oikonomos* in the church has a gift or gifts. He, too, is judged a "good" steward on the basis of his effective use of those gifts in service to others.

(5) Christians are stewards of the "manifold" grace of God.

The grace of God is evidenced in creation and redemption. In the assembly of the saints that grace of God is also apparent in the spiritual gifts. Lists of such gifts occur in the New Testament in Ephesians 4:11-13; Romans 12:4-8, First Corinthians 12:1-11; 12:28-31. In the combination of these lists at least twenty-one different gifts are named.

1. Apostles	12. Discerning of spirits
2. Prophets	13. Tongues
3. Evangelists	14. Interpretation of tongues
4. Pastors	15. Ministry
5. Teachers	16. Exhortation
6. Words of wisdom	17. Giving
7. Words of knowledge	18. Ruling
8. Faith	19. Helps
9. Healing	20. Governments
10. Miracles	21. Celibacy (1 Cor. 7:7)
11. Prophecy	

These expressions of God's grace in "grace gifts" may or may not be exhaustive. But without doubt they do demonstrate the "manifold" nature of the grace of God.

Verse 11. Generally, all of the above-mentioned gifts are expressed in one of two ways. Either they are verbal gifts or they are ministering gifts. Verbal gifts have to do with the presentation of the gospel and the teaching of the tenets of Christ. Gifts such as apostles, prophets, teachers, words of wisdom, and tongues fall in this category. The ministering gifts included healing, ministry, and helps. Some, such as pastors, seem to be at home in either category. The apostle recognizes that the gifts fall naturally into these two broad categories and proceeds to speak of the manner of their discharge.

When one is speaking, let him speak as one who utters God's words. "Oracles" is *logia*, and, according to Bigg, the reference is to Scripture. "The Christians' talk is to be modelled on the Bible."[7] Support for Bigg's thesis could be mar-

---

[7]Bigg, *Commentary on St. Peter and St. Jude*, p. 174.

shalled from Romans 3:1-2 where Paul argues that the Jews enjoy the advantage of having the "oracles of God" *(logia tou theou)* committed or entrusted to them. Doubtless, Paul's reference was to Scripture.

Selwyn thinks that the reference is not to the Bible, but to the act of preaching. This does seem more in keeping with the context of the use of spiritual gifts. If this is correct, then "the teacher or preacher is not to be the purveyor of his own notions, but the transmitter of the utterances of God. . . ."[8] Whichever is the case, the passage makes it clear that the use of the utterance gifts is to be in accord at all times with the mind and purpose of God.

The service gifts are also emphasized. If one "ministers" *(diakonei)*, he is to do so, not in the strength and motivation of the flesh, but in the "ability which God giveth." That last word is *chorēgeō*. Selwyn notes:

> *Chorēgein* meant initially 'to be a chorus leader'; then, since actor-managers became more common, 'to supply a chorus' and so produce a play at one's own risk; and finally, . . . simply to furnish or supply anything.[9]

God supplies both motivation and strength for the effective ministering of the grace gifts to the congregation.

However, there is another goal which towers above the task of ministry to the churches. That goal is that God the Father may be glorified through Jesus Christ. The way in which this works is as follows: Normal human behavior dictates the exposure and condemnation of failure. Furthermore, depravity guarantees a selfish tendency in man that makes him liable to the use of spiritual gifts in a selfish fashion.

But when the Holy Spirit changes the heart in the new birth, He creates a desire to imitate the life of Christ. The disciple loves fervently, thus covering a multitude of sins, and

---

[8]Selwyn, *First Epistle of Saint Peter,* p. 219.
[9]*Ibid.*

brings glory to God by demonstrating tl e spiritual power of the reborn soul.

By the same token, Jesus was the ultimate servant in His voluntary death on the cross. As the church inculcates that Spirit of Christ in the use of ministering gifts, it brings glory to the Father, the one to whom is ascribed all glory and dominion forever and forever. This doxology into which Peter has broken concludes with the autnor's own hearty "Amen." The word which derived originally from Hebrew is a term of affirmation. Peter simply voices his own agreement to the exalted presentation of the Lord.

Fiery Trials

---

1. Unanticipated Trials (4:12-13)
2. Unashamed Sufferings (4:14-16)
3. Ungodly Destinies (4:17-18)
4. Unfailing Providences (4:19)

Author's Translation (4:12-19)

12—Beloved, do not be amazed at the fiery trial which is coming among you to test you, as something strange happening to you.

13—But to the degree that you go on sharing the sufferings of Christ, rejoice, so that also, at the revelation of His glory, you yourselves might rejoice, celebrating exceedingly.

14—If you are reviled because of the name of Christ, blessed [are you], because the Spirit of Glory and the Spirit of God rests upon you.

15—For let not any of you suffer as a murderer, or a thief, or an evildoer, or as one who meddles in the affairs of other men.

16—But if [one suffers] as a Christian, let him not be ashamed, but in this name let him continually glorify God.

17—Because [it is] time for judgment to begin from the house of God; but if with us first, what [will be] the destiny for those who are refusing to be persuaded of the good news of God?

18—And if the righteous with difficulty are being saved, where shall the ungodly and the sinner appear?

19—Consequently, also the ones who are suffering with reference to the will of God, let them continually entrust their souls [in doing good] to the faithful creator.

Unanticipated Trials (4:12-13)

12—Beloved, think it not strange concerning the fiery trial which is to try you, as though some strange thing happened unto you;

13—But rejoice, inasmuch as ye are partakers of Christ's sufferings; that, when his glory shall be revealed, ye may be glad also with exceeding joy.

The theme of suffering returns to prominence in the last segment of the fourth chapter. This time Peter not only anticipates the inevitable nature of suffering but also suggests that such circumstances should not develop as a surprise to the brethren. In verses 12-13, Peter discusses the unanticipated trials. Then, in verses 14-16, the shame normally associated with the suffering of persecution is addressed. God's intervention in judgment, especially regarding the destinies of the ungodly, is the topic of verses 17-18. Finally, the unfailing providences of God are recounted in verse 19.

Verse 12. The recipients are addressed in a gentle, affectionate, and pastoral way, wonderfully appropriate to the announcement of imminent trial. They are called "beloved," indicating the intensity of the fisherman-apostle's love for these brethren. The counsel is then offered that they are not to be startled, amazed, or to view as strange the approaching trials. The Lord had made this same point to the disciples when he cautioned them, reminding them that the same ones who hated Him would despise His followers also (Mark 13:13).

Three general truths are distinguishable in the text. First, trials will happen. Second, not all trials will be mild and passing difficulties, but fiery encounters. Third, at least a portion of the purpose will be the testing of the believer. Trials will "happen."

That last word is a translation of *sumbainō*. *Bainō* means "to stand," while *sun* is a preposition meaning "together." The word often envisioned two parties meeting to discuss differences and, hopefully, to arrive at a compromise. Gradually it simply adopted the idea of "coming together" in the sense of "happening" as used here. The Christian, by virtue of his profession, is on a collision course with suffering. The world is antagonistic to the saint's commitment.

These encounters are described by Peter as "fiery." This rare word, used only here and twice in Revelation, focuses on the severity of the testings. A chronicle of the sufferings of Paul (2 Cor. 11:21-28) or of the heroes of the faith (Heb. 11:32-40) provides insight into the extent of these expected tribulations. The purpose for these sufferings is in part the matter of testing. Swiss theologian Karl Barth wrote,

> What we are and have and think and do and attempt as Christians in good days, when the situation is calm and favorable and we are not exposed to any serious assaults from within or without, is always subject, for all its conscious zeal and sincerity, to the difficult question whether and how far it is tested, and hardened, and solid and enduring.[1]

In other words, the trials not only provide witness to onlookers concerning the adequacy of our faith, they even assist in demonstrating for the benefit of the one being tested that the Lord is able to meet every need in the fiery furnace. The three Hebrew children would probably not have enjoyed the company of the one "like unto the son of man" if they had not been in the furnace for God's sake.

Verse 13. Not only is suffering the occasion for testing, it also provides opportunity for rejoicing. Peter is not proposing an absurd delight in the pangs of affliction per se. But he is recognizing that the presence of such sorrows enables the believer to become a participant in Christ's sufferings. Participating in the sufferings of Jesus does not mean that there is anything propitiatory about the sufferings of the saints. Nothing needs to be added to the atonement of Christ. His death at Golgotha is wholly sufficient. F. B. Meyer spoke of this.

---

[1] Karl Barth, *Church Dogmatics*, vol. IV, Part 2, p. 609.

Meyer further appeals to the incident recorded in Second Samuel 15:21 as an example of what is here intended. Ittai the Gittite says, "As the Lord liveth . . . surely in what place my lord the king shall be, whether in death or life, even there also will thy servant be" (2 Sam. 15:21). The idea is that the saints follow their king. On earth that means traversing the barren wastes of persecution.

> Of course there is a sense in which Christ's sufferings are unapproachable. They stand as a solitary obelisk on the sands of time.[2]

Rejoicing is in order because the disciple knows that as he successfully negotiates the ravages of tribulation, he will also experience "exceeding joy" at the return of Christ. The return of Jesus is presented in terms of "when His glory shall be revealed." "Revealed" is a translation of the word *apokalupsis*, from which the English word "apocalypse" is derived. Literally, it refers to an unveiling. In the incarnation, the humanity of Jesus in a sense veiled His deity. The closest approximation to the glory yet to be revealed was at the transfiguration. The day is coming when the glorified Christ shall be unveiled before the entire cosmos. It is this event to which the apostle refers. For many the event will be sorrowful and terrifying (see Rev. 6:16). But for the Christian, it will be a time of indescribable joy.

Unashamed Sufferings (4:14-16)

14—If ye be reproached for the name of Christ, happy are ye; for the spirit of glory and of God resteth upon you: on their part he is evil spoken of, but on your part he is glorified.

15—But let none of you suffer as a murderer, or as a thief, or as an evildoer, or as a busybody in other men's matters.

16—Yet if any man suffer as a Christian, let him not be ashamed; but let him glorify God on this behalf.

---

[2]Meyer, *Tried by Fire*, p. 155.

Verse 14. The specific nature of some of these trials is now delineated. The instance in view is the suffering of reproach. The word thus translated is *oneidizō* and means "to censure" or "to insult with opprobrious language." While the precise origin of this word is not known, evidence is strong that it derives from an Indo-European root, *neid*, which means "revile."[3] The reproach suffered has to do with the name of Christ. The conclusion drawn about such persecutions is a reminiscence of the Lord's own words in the Beatitudes. "Happy are ye" is the translation. "Are ye" is in italics in the King James Version indicating that they have been added. Actually, the word *makarioi* stands alone again just as it did in 3:14.

Whereas the cause of jubilation in 4:13 was the joy of the Lord's return, the happiness promised in verse 14 is based upon the presence of the Spirit of glory and of God that rests now on the believer. The profound joy of the Christian awaits full realization when the fullness of Christ's glory is revealed at His return. But a harbinger of that glory resides with the believer now. The language is similar to the Old Testament texts that relate the coming of the glory cloud, the *shekinah*, as the rabbis called it. When the *shekinah* or cloud of glory fell upon the tabernacle or temple, the priests could not minister because of the presence of God. While Peter does not forecast any such visible demonstration for his hearers, the "Spirit" of that glory, namely, the Spirit of God rests upon them.

The reproach of men for Christ's sake became the object of rejoicing, first, because one knows that it is obvious to his persecutors that the Spirit of God rests upon him. Second, the cause for rejoicing is present because, in the very agonies of persecution, the Spirit of God makes known His presence resting in power upon the sufferer. The last phrase of the verse is absent from most of the better manuscripts. Whether or not it was part of Peter's original composition, the state-

---

[3]Kittel, *Theological Dictionary*, vol. V, p. 238.

ment is accurate. While men may speak evil of Christ, the actions of His followers exhibit the glory of Christ to the extent that evil talk is made ludicrous.

Verse 15. Four categories comprise a list of offenses for which godly men ought never to suffer. Three of the four are clear and predictable. The fourth is unique. The first category, murder, is thought by some commentators to be a reference to the social practice of exposing unwanted infants. If so, then the prohibition concerns one of the ancient equivalents to modern abortion, though the latter was also practiced in the world of antiquity. The idea seems to be that no Christian could possibly be guilty of homicide. More probable is the view that a general reverence for life, recognizing that man is not the author of life and that he has no right to take life, is in the apostle's mind. Apparently, Peter anticipates the possibility of suffering the same kind of penalty for following Christ as that which would befall a convicted murderer, but he urges the injustice of the action and cautions that the believer is to do nothing worthy of capital punishment.

"Thief" is *kleptēs* from which the English word "kleptomania" is partially derived. This is the second offense. The stricture against suffering as a thief is an indication that God allows and even encourages ownership and possessions. He moves, as He always has, to protect the rights of possession. Besides the disciple need not steal since God will supply all his needs (Phil. 4:19). Third, "evildoer" marks a return to one of Peter's favorite descriptive terms, *kakos*. Here it is an all-encompassing term, designed to cover any moral failure not more specifically stated earlier.

The last forbidden activity is interestingly translated as a prohibition of the believer's becoming "a busybody in other men's matters." The actual word employed may well have been coined by Peter since it is a *hapax legomena*, a case of only one appearance in the New Testament. Furthermore, Liddell and Scott list no other occurrence of the word in secular Greek, though there are similar cases of compound words utilizing part of the same expression. The expression is *allotriepiskopos*, which literally means "to oversee the activities of another." The word combines the word translated elsewhere as "bishop" *(episkopos)* with the adjective "another."

Selwyn thinks this may be a reference to tactless attempts to convert others. While Peter would not sanction tactlessness in evangelism, surely this is not at all what he has in mind. Confronting men with the claims of Christ will always appear to some to be void of tact.

In this case, the etymology of the word is probably the best index to its significance. The King James translation may be quaint, but still accurate. Few nuisances are any more repulsive than someone who meddles in the affairs of others, especially since such persons usually exhibit a notable lack of attention to their own problems. The suffering engendered by such meddling would not be as ominous as that mentioned for earlier crimes, but the true believer ought not to suffer even the neglect or the rebuke brought about by unnecessary intrusion into other men's affairs.

Verse 16. In the event that one suffers as a Christian, he should not feel the shame associated with public punishment. In colonial New England, the idea involved in public chastisement was not so much to inflict pain as to assess public humiliation and shame. However, suffering for Christ should be free of shame.

The use of the word "Christian" is somewhat startling. Luke employs the term twice in Acts, including the famous reference to the first use of the word in Antioch (Acts 11:36). Otherwise, as common as the word is in modern parlance, it is used only here in the New Testament. The meaning is "little Christs." Because of the commonplace frequence of this word, it has lost much of it actual impact. To early readers, the word as used both here and in Acts must have generated an almost electric response.

The King James text fails to reflect that excitement in the translation of the last phrase of the verse. "Let him glorify

God on this behalf" is better rendered literally "let him glorify God by this name." The very name "Christian," perhaps used reproachfully as a mockery, should become a method of bringing glory to God. In being called Christians, these saints were labeled as belonging to Christ and, hopefully, as ones exhibiting the spirit of Christ in their lives.

Ungodly Destinies (4:17-18)

17—For the time is come that judgment must begin at the house of God: and if it first begin at us, what shall the end be of them that obey not the gospel of God?

18—And if the righteous scarcely be saved, where shall the ungodly and the sinner appear?

Verse 17. The verse before us apparently has been formed by joining Jeremiah 25:29 and Ezekiel 9:6. The background, particularly of the Ezekiel reference, is the onslaught of the armies of Babylon against rebellious Jerusalem. The glory of God has departed from the temple and Ezekiel quotes God as instructing the Babylonians to "slay utterly old and young" and to "begin at my sanctuary." The prophecy anticipates the last hours of the fall of Jerusalem to Nebuchadnezzar. Many who had disregarded God altogether sought sanctuary in the temple, supposing that God would spare them in that sacred precinct. God says to begin the judgment of His people in His sanctuary.

Peter's application of this to the first century takes a different turn. The verses are not unrelated to the admonitions about suffering which precede them. The persecutions which the saints must face will have a purifying and pruning effect similar to that of the Babylonian captivity's effect upon Israel. "Judgment" *(krima)* probably has the significance of judgment ensuing in both positive and negative conclusions, but not in the sense of "condemnation."

The larger question is now broached. If God so examines

His own people, "the house of God," what then shall the end be like for those who have disobeyed the gospel? The background of Ezekiel's prophecy is still in Peter's mind, together with the awareness of what God may allow Christians to suffer for Christ's name. If these judgments of God assume such devastating proportions for believers, what shall the *telos*, the consummation, be for those who have chosen disobedience to the gospel? The question does not necessitate a precise response. Obviously, the answer is incalculable sorrow.

Verse 18. The question of verse 17 is now phrased in terms of salvation rather than of judgment. The query is almost identical to Solomon's declaration in Proverbs 11:31. In fact, this is a near quote of the Septuagint version of Proverbs 11:31. If the righteous "scarcely" are saved, where will the ungodly and the sinner appear? "Scarcely" translates *molis*, which basically means "copious labor." The concept is not of works salvation but of "unlikely" salvation or salvation appropriated with great difficulty. Only God can save. Man's finest efforts falter. As John Newton wrote:

> Beyond a doubt, I rest assured
> Thou are the Christ of God;
> Who has eternal life secured
> promise and by blood.
>
> The help of men and angels join'd
> Could never reach my case;
> Nor can I hope relief to find
> But in thy boundless grace.

C. H. Spurgeon reminded his congregation:

> Do you not, dear brethren and sisters in Christ, sometimes feel how hard it is for you to be saved, when you put your soul before the tribunal of your own enlightened conscience? Our own conscience, at the best, is a poor partial judge compared

with the impartial and infallible Judge who will, by and by, sit upon the great white throne. . . .[4]

The difficulty of salvation is not found in any limitation or insufficiency in the work of Christ. The difficulty is found in restraining the just wrath of God against sin. The severity of this affronted holiness is observable in the death of Jesus on the cross. While all men deserve condemnation, those who come to Christ escape that judgment. But since these "scarcely" are saved, what will happen to the ungodly and the unrepentant sinner? Again this is a rhetorical question, the response to which is a shaking of the head.

Unfailing Providences (4:19)

19—Wherefore let them that suffer according to the will of God commit the keeping of their souls to him in well doing, as unto a faithful Creator.

Verse 19. The subject now returns to the temporal suffering of Christians. Peter's concluding word on the subject is an appeal to trust the providences of a beneficent God. Believers suffering justly cannot exercise the option which the apostle here suggests. Believers who suffer with reference to the will of God are encouraged to commit the keeping of their souls in well-doing to the Creator. "Commit" is the translation of *paratithesthosan* which derives from *tithemi,* meaning "to place," and *para,* meaning "beside" or "with." Christians are to place their souls with the faithful Creator.

Three aspects are important here. First, the souls of men are to be placed with the Creator. The use of the word "Creator" clearly suggests power and authority. If God made all that exists, surely He possesses the power to sustain His creation. Particularly will He care for His children (5:7). But He is also the "faithful" Creator. This does not indicate that He

---

[4]C. H. Spurgeon, *The Metropolitan Tabernacle Pulpit,* vol. LIII, p. 329.

faithfully creates, although this is not untrue. Rather, the emphasis is that the one who is the Creator continues faithful in preserving those who trust Him. Finally, the method of demonstrating the commitment of our souls to the faithful Creator is by means of the doing of good works.

Crowns for Shepherds

1. The Crown of Glory (5:1-4)
2. The Clothing of Humility (5:5-7)
3. The Crisis of Resistance (5:8-11)
4. The Church of Babylon (5:12-14)

Author's Translation (5:1-14)

1—Therefore, I exhort the elders among you [as] fellow-elder and witness of the sufferings of Christ, and a sharer in the glory which is about to be revealed,

2—Shepherd the flock of God among you, not overseeing unwillingly, but voluntarily with reference to God, not for the sake of gain but cheerfully,

3—Not as one who is acting as lord over those allotted to you but become models for the flock.

4—And when the chief Shepherd is made manifest you will receive the unfading victor's crown of glory.

5—In a similar way, younger men, be subjected to the elders and all be clothed with humility toward one another, because God, himself, resists the arrogant, but gives grace to the humble.

6—Humble yourselves, therefore, under the mighty hand of God, in order that He may exalt you in time.

7—Casting all your care upon Him, because He, Himself, cares for you.

8—Be vigilant, be watchful. Your adversary, the devil, continues to prowl about as a roaring lion, seeking someone to devour.

9—Whom you oppose, stedfast in the faith, knowing that the same sufferings are endured by your brethren in the world.

10—But the God of all grace, the one who called you unto His eternal glory in Christ, after you have suffered a little, will Himself perfect, confirm, strengthen, and establish [you].

11—To Him be dominion unto the ages, amen.

12—By Silvanus, a faithful brother to you, as I regard [him], through whom I have written briefly, exhorting and testifying this to be the true grace of God; in which you stand.

13—She who is in Babylon sends greetings, chosen together with you, and Mark, my son.

14—Greet one another with a kiss of love. Peace be unto all who are in Christ.

The Crown of Glory (5:1-4)

1—The elders which are among you I exhort, who am also an elder, and a witness of the sufferings of Christ, and also a partaker of the glory that shall be revealed:

2—Feed the flock of God which is among you, taking the oversight thereof, not by constraint, but willingly; not for filthy lucre, but of a ready mind;

3—Neither as being lords over God's heritage, but being examples to the flock.

4—And when the chief Shepherd shall appear, ye shall receive a crown of glory that fadeth not away.

The concluding chapter of First Peter encompasses the expected specific greetings (which are generally located at the conclusion of ancient Near Eastern letters), pastoral advice, and some marvelous promises. The work of a pastor, including his crown of glory, is the subject of verses 1-4. The necessity of putting on the clothing of humility is the consideration in verses 5-7. The crisis of resistance occupies the apostle's mind in verses 8-11. The last section brings a salutation from the church of Babylon (vv. 12-14).

Verse 1. In the first two verses of this chapter is an insight into early ecclesiology which is crucial for the modern church. Three words are employed in the two verses to describe the role of a pastor. In verse 1, he is called an "elder" *(presbuteros).* In verse 2 he is asked to "shepherd" *(poimainō)* the flock, taking oversight *(episkopountes)* of the congregation. "Elder" is a noun, while the other two words are verbs in this text. However, they are used elsewhere in the New Testament in their nominal forms, *poimēn* (Eph. 4:11) and *episkopos* (1 Tim. 3:2), to describe the same office. First, we must draw conclusions about the spiritual leadership of the church in the apostolic era and then devote our attention to the significance of each title.

The early church was a priesthood of believers, as Peter has already indicated in 2:4-10. This doctrine was one of rare privilege and ominous responsibility. But leadership is necessary. Accordingly, the early churches operated with pastors and deacons as spiritual leaders. If Acts 6:1-7 can be construed as the appointing of the original diaconate, then it is possible to delineate accurately the division of duties. According to Acts 6:4, the apostles, who were, in effect, in the role of pastors, were to devote themselves to the study and teaching of the word of God and to the ministry of prayer. Deacons, while possessing high spiritual qualifications, were to minister to the physical necessities of the burgeoning church. *There is no justification for the diaconate serving as a business operation or decision-making body for the church.* To the contrary, the word *diakonia* stipulates a "servant," a "table waiter." If any position was heralded as a major decision-making or ruling task, it was that of the pastor (Heb. 13:7,17).

The work of the pastor is described by three terms which all refer to the same individual but are not strictly synonymous in that they each describe a facet of the pastoral office. *Presbuteros* means "elder" and has a generic meaning and a technically derived significance. Mature men blessed of God with advanced years are called "elders". The ancient Near East honored the elderly in much the same way as they are honored in a society like Japan today. The word "elder" was a term of respect and esteem. As such, the word was employed by the early church to describe its pastoral leaders, even though they were, on occasion, very young. "Elder" becomes the expression describing the high esteem accorded by the church to those who held the pastoral office.

The other words, *poimēn* and *episkopos*, are functional descriptions. "Pastor" *(poimēn)* means "shepherd" and is descriptive of the spiritual assignments of the congregational leader. He is the man charged with feeding and protecting the sheep as well as presiding over the birth of new lambs. "Shepherd" depicts his role as a spiritual leader. W. A. Criswell remarks, "The imagery of a shepherd and flock was deep in the hearts of the people of Israel. Being a shepherd was an exalted vocation, and the reason for it is evident, for the patriarchs were shepherds."[1] "Bishop" *(episkopos)* means "overseer" and refers to the administrative functions of the elder. The concept of the "bishop" is not the idea of a pastoral office exercising diocesan control over numerous churches and their clergy. Rather, it is local bishops' exercising administrative leadership in their respective individual churches. In summary, "elder" is a term indicating the esteem in which the office is held (1 Tim. 5:1,17,19). "Bishop" accentuates the administrative responsibilities of the elder, while "pastor" or "shepherd" focuses on the spiritual ministries of the elder (Eph. 4:11).

Clearly, the early church had a plurality of elders (Acts 20:17). These spiritual leaders doubtless served their local congregations in a variety of ministries which were dictated, at least partially, by the spiritual gifts which each possessed. For example, some would be involved mostly in evangelism, while others would devote themselves to teaching ministries. But all of these elders were called "pastors" and "bishops" as well. Some have imagined that "elders" are a separate category from "pastors." This fails to note the obvious interchangeability of these terms. Furthermore, why are there no qualifications in First Timothy 3 for the elder? Bishops and deacons are specifically mentioned, but elders are absent from the text.

---

[1]W. A. Criswell, *Expository Sermons on the Epistles of Peter*, p. 92.

Even among the elders of a church, evidently there was one who was the evident spiritual leader of the church. Ephesus had "elders" but John was almost certainly *the pastor* until his exile on Patmos. God has almost always worked through individuals rather than committees. While the pastoral office may not have carried the same authority as the apostolic office, it is clear that the circumstances are similar and that the pastoral office was to predominate after the exodus of the apostles.

Peter addresses the elders of the diaspora churches as one who is also an elder. Further, he is a witness to the sufferings of Christ and a partaker of the glory which is about to be revealed. How vivid must have been the picture of Christ's passion, indelibly imprinted on Peter's mind. The numerous references to the atonement in this short epistle provide some insight to the impact of the whole experience. Peter is also a "partaker" *(koinōnos)* of the glory about to be revealed. The word *koinōnos* refers to "things held in common." For example, the Greek New Testament is written in *koinē* Greek as opposed to the classical Greek of Plato or Aristotle. That is, the New Testament is written in the "common language," the vernacular of the market place, not the lofty literary excellencies which would to some degree elude the common man. Therefore, Peter identifies himself as belonging to a segment of society which will "share" the glory which is about to be revealed. See 4:14 for a reference to glory and 5:4 for a reference to the glory about to be revealed.

Verse 2. The controlling verb for the instructions of verse 2 is in verse 1. "I exhort" means "I call to my side" in this endeavor. The tasks to which Peter summons them are "feeding" and "taking the oversight," the two primary tasks of the elders. "Feed" is an accurate translation of *poimainō,* but not a good one. "Feeding" the flock, teaching them the truths of God, is certainly the major assignment. The translator's task is complicated by the fact that "pastor" and "shepherd" are nouns. Until recently there was no corresponding verb for "pastor" and rarely was "shepherd" used as a verb. However, an adequate translation of this mandate would be "pastor the flock" or "shepherd the flock," thus including all of the above mentioned facets of the duties of a shepherd.

This shepherdly assignment relates specifically to the flock of God "which is among you." Two notable avowals emerge here. First, it is God's flock which the shepherd tends, not his own. Many a pastor forgets this, abusing the sheep which God has committed to his hand. Second, the flock is not the universal church or even a conglomerate of several congregations. These shepherds are limited to responsibility for the local flock, the one which is with and around them.

"Taking the oversight," *episkopountes*, might be rendered "being bishop," though the King James translation is quite good here. The bishops are instructed to labor neither by "constraint" nor "for filthy lucre." "Constraint" is an adverb which indicates necessity and sometimes even "moral duty." The antonym is another adverb, "willingly," which is associated with voluntarism as opposed to conscription. Not only is the pastor to accept his work spontaneously, but also he is to do so in the state of "a ready mind" as opposed to that of seeking "filthy lucre."

The phrase "of a ready mind" translates only one Greek word, *prothumōs*. This word in turn derives from *thumos* which, as mentioned earlier, originally was associated with a violent movement of, for example, water or air. Gradually, it became associated with the concept of anger. However, the original significance of "violent movement" is sometimes retained in a word like *prothumōs*. The prefix *pro* means "before" or "in advance of." The word *prothumōs* came to mean "vigorous approach from the first." The translation "of a ready mind" is too mild to catch the spirit of the phrase. "Vigorously from the first" might come closer to capturing the idea.

The prohibition added to the "not of constraint" limitation is that the pastor will not labor for "filthy lucre," the quaint and colorful King James translation of *aischrokerdōs*. The last part of the word *kerdos*, simply means "gain." The first part (*aischros*) indicates "dishonorable" or "indecorous."

The stipulation does not suggest that the pastor is not to receive a stipend, even a very generous one. Paul, for example, insists that those who preach the gospel should be sustained by those who are the recipients of that ministry (1 Cor. 9:9,14). The prohibition here is twofold. First, the work of a pastor is not to receive its motivation from the hope of monetary profit. Whereas a business endeavor can have, as one of its legitimate goals, the acquisition of wealth, the pastor can never allow such a goal to affect his ministry in any way. Second, acquisition of support which involved compromise of any kind is also prohibited. Wealth accumulated at the cost of conviction or truth would thus become dishonorable gain.

One other technical point must be mentioned in this verse. The word *episkopountes*, "taking oversight," is of questionable textual support. For example, both Codex Sinaiticus and Vaticanus omit the word. These are two of the better ancient texts. On the other hand, p^{72}, a third-century Bodmer papyrus, sustains the word. No doctrine is affected by the deletion of the word. However, that early papyrus reference together with a host of other evidences is sufficient to establish a high probability for including the word.

Verse 3. The author of Hebrews views the pastor from the perspective of the congregation. Hence, his language in Hebrews 13:7,17 is strong, ascribing to the spiritual leader the role of a ruler. Peter's view of that same pastoral office is from the perspective of the pastor. If the people are to see the pastor as a ruler, the pastor is to view himself as a servant. Trouble begins when one or both reverse those role assignments. A pastor who exalts himself as ruler is an unbearable anomaly. A flock which views its shepherd as its slave is destined for spiritual disaster.

Verse 3 is a continuation of Peter's instruction for elders. Not only are they to shepherd the flock cheerfully and spontaneously, but also they are to refrain from playing the role of "lord." "As being lords" is a translation of a vivid Greek compound word *katakurieuontes*. The preposition *kata*, meaning "down," is attached to the verb *kurieuō*, meaning "to master." Thus the idea emerges of one who is master over another. The shepherd is not the master over the flock. The flock belongs to God, and the shepherd is God's appointed watchman. This ownership of the flock is emphasized by reference to God's "heritage." "Heritage" is *klēros* which, according to Selwyn, meant "an allotment of land assigned to a citizen by the civic authorities."[2] So God's "heritage" has been assigned to the shepherds for safekeeping.

How then is the shepherd to view his own role? He is to be an example *(tupos)* for the flock. This word *tupos* was already observed in 3:21 in one of its forms as *antitupos*. The English word "type" is actually a loan word from Greek. The idea is that the life and attitudes of the pastor are to be a model for the flock to imitate. The awesomeness of this responsibility is breathtaking. A pastor may expect to reproduce himself to a significant degree in his sheep.

Verse 4. The reward for which the pastor labors is one that will only be presented when the chief Shepherd appears. There are, of course, wonderful rewards for the pastor in terms of changed lives and the privileges associated with the preaching of the word. But the ultimate reward for the preacher is one provided directly by the chief Shepherd. In fact there is an observable contrast between the "dishonorable gain" of verse 2 and the chief Shepherd's reward in verse 4. The gain of verse 2 is temporal and thus subject to decay; it is limited; and it is provided by men. The reward of verse 4 is eternal, incorruptible, unlimited, and it is provided by the Savior.

The drift of the entire passage is that the pastor is not to be preoccupied with earthly profit but is to labor for the heavenly reward. This will be provided when the chief Shepherd, an obvious reference to Jesus, shall appear. Five words are frequently employed in the New Testament to describe the return of Christ. The word used here is *phaneroō*. Else-

---

[2]Selwyn, *First Epistle of Saint Peter*, p. 231.

where, *parousia* (1 Cor. 15:23), *epiphaneia* (2 Thess. 2:8), *apokalupsis* (1 Cor. 15:23), or *erchomai* (Heb. 10:37) will be used. The general meaning is the same though there is a distinction in emphasis.

Erchomai is the general word for "coming."

Epiphaneia means "glorious display."

Parousia means "presence."

Apokalupsis means "to unveil."

Phaneroō means "to disclose" or "to make manifest."

Notably absent from this terminology is the frequently used modern phrase "second coming." This phrase is never employed in the Scriptures. The closest approximation to it is found in Hebrews 9:28, which says that Christ will appear "a second time." Because of Theophanies or Christophanies, it is best to speak of the "incarnation" of Christ rather than of His "first coming." Likewise, it is best to speak of His "return" rather than of His "second coming." The words used in the New Testament to describe this event show that Christ will "come" *(erchomai)* just as before to be "present" *(parousia)* with us. This will constitute a "disclosure" *(phaneroō)* of His glory and a "revelation" *(apokalupsis)* of His person which will be a dazzling "display" *(epiphaneia)* of heavenly power and splendor.

This is the event which Peter and all genuine shepherds eagerly await. When the Archshepherd is disclosed, then faithful shepherds will receive crowns of glory which never fade. Two kinds of crowns are mentioned in the New Testament. The *diadēma*, or diadem, is the kingly crown worn by Christ (Rev. 19:12). The *stephanos*, or victor's crown, is that which is awarded to the servants of Christ at His coming. Five such *stephanoi* are mentioned by name.

(1) An incorruptible crown given for mastery over the flesh (see 1 Cor. 9:25).

(2) A crown of rejoicing for those who win men to Christ (see 1 Thess. 2:19).

(3) A crown of life for those who suffer tribulation (see James 1:12; Rev. 2:10).

(4) A crown of righteousness for those who love His appearing (see 2 Tim. 4:8).

(5) An unfading crown for faithful shepherds (see 1 Peter 5:4).

The point here is not to become preoccupied with the subject of rewards in general or crowns in particular. Perhaps all of the above represent the same crown with the specific descriptions given to show some of the activities which God particularly honors. In any case, Peter is certain that the work of the pastor is to be performed against the backdrop of the return of Christ and the unfading reward which He shall bring.

The Clothing of Humility (5:5-7)

5—Likewise, ye younger, submit yourselves unto the elder. Yea, all of you be subject one to another, and be clothed with humility: for God resisteth the proud, and giveth grace to the humble.

6—Humble yourselves therefore under the mighty hand of God, that he may exalt you in due time:

7—Casting all your care upon him; for he careth for you.

Verse 5. The discussion of the humility of the pastor leads the apostle to a general discussion of humility. First, the younger men are to submit themselves to their elders. "Submission" is the same concept discussed in an earlier passage. It employs voluntary acquiescence based on the recognition of the younger men that the elders possessed experiential knowledge which the younger men did not have. However, there is another aspect of submission which becomes apparent in the next admonition. Each is asked to be submissive to everyone else. Here it becomes apparent that the matter of authority is not so much in the thinking of Simon Peter as is the attitude of humility.

This becomes obvious when he speaks of being "clothed" with humility. The expression "clothed" is *egkombōsasthe*, a word which occurs only here in the New Testament. Ellicott refers to it as a "rare and curious" verb. He translates the verb, "Tie yourself up in humility." He further states that the reference is to a cape which was worn only by slaves.[3] Liddell and Scott verify this, referring to the *egkombōma* as "a frock or apron" worn by slaves in the discharge of menial duties.[4] Doubtless, the picture indelibly impressed in Peter's mind is of Jesus, clothed with a towel *(lention)* as a slave, washing the feet of His disciples. The kind of submission to one another which is demanded is that of profound humility taken to oneself like a garment.

To provide further impetus to the admonition, Peter appeals to the Septuagint translation of Proverbs 3:34. God resists the proud. "Resists" is probably a play on words with "submit" in the earlier part of the verse. "Submit" is *hupotassō* while "resist" is *antitassomai*. If men do not "place" themselves in humility "under" one another, then God "places" Himself "against" them. "Proud" translates the Greek word *huperēphanos*, which combines the verb "to appear" and the preposition "over." One who appears to be over the rest would merit the designation "proud."

Verse 6. While God resists the proud, He gives grace to the humble. Therefore, all believers should humble themselves under the mighty hand of God, realizing that at the proper time God will exalt them. Note that Peter speaks of the "mighty hand" of God. God's hand is irresistible. Why, then, would anyone challenge Him? In time *(kairos)*, God will exalt the humble. The word *kairos* is used rather than *chronos*, indicating that the time in view is distinctively God's choice of time.

Verse 7. Again, the humility enjoined upon the reader is not so much general humility, though this, too, is desirable. It is rather a humility in the face of the fiery trials that Peter has

---

[3]Charles John Ellicott, *Ellicott's Commentary on the Whole Bible*, vol. VIII, p. 433.

[4]Liddell and Scott, *Greek-English Lexicon*, p. 473.

already prognosticated. Thus humility is exhibited through non-retaliation against persecutors and the casting of all care upon Him. "Care" refers to "anxious interest" or "deep concerns." This word is *merimna* and is different from the word used in the last phrase, "He careth [*melei*] for you." Even so, the idea is that our anxieties can be cast upon Him because the God of the mighty hand cares what happens to us.

The Crisis of Resistance (5:8-11)

8—Be sober, be vigilant; because your adversary the devil, as a roaring lion, walketh about, seeking whom he may devour:

9—Whom resist steadfast in the faith, knowing that the same afflictions are accomplished in your brethren that are in the world.

10—But the God of all grace, who hath called us unto his eternal glory by Christ Jesus, after that ye have suffered a while, make you perfect, stablish, strengthen, settle you.

11—To him be glory and dominion for ever and ever. Amen.

Verse 8. Sobriety and vigilance or watchfulness are suggested for the saints in light of the activities of Satan. Satan is called the adversary (*antidikos*) which Stibbs says refers normally to "an opponent in a lawsuit."[5] He is also called the devil (*diabolos*), a word which literally means "to cast through" and hence "to slander." John Brown remarks that "the attacks of our great spiritual enemy naturally divide themselves into two classes; those which are made on the Christian as an individual, and those which are made on the Christian cause."[6] In a sense, Satan is more in the role of adversary to the cause and as accuser of the individual Christian. However, these activities overlap.

The devil is described as pacing about impatiently like a roaring lion. "Roaring," a classic case of onomatopoeia, is the Greek word *ōruomenos*, which sounds like what it is, i.e.,

---

[5]Alan M. Stibbs, *The First Epistle General of Peter*, p. 172.
[6]John Brown, *Expository Discourses on I Peter*, vol. 2, p. 572.

"roaring." The purpose of this frantic and threatening behavior on the part of Satan is to seek those whom he might devour. The last word translates *katapinō*. With the preposition *kata*, meaning "down," prefixed to the verb "to eat," the expression might be translated as "eat down," which is more accurate physiologically than the English expression "eat up." In any case, the purpose of Satan is to consume the believer, immersing him in evil and guilt and thus frustrating whatever usefulness he might have for the work of the kingdom.

Verse 9. The methods of dealing with Satan are outlined clearly. In verse 8, "sobriety" suggests full awareness of the person and work of Satan. Two mistakes can be made in this regard. Some become enchanted with the study of demonology. Paul cautions that our major thoughts are to be stayed upon the things that are true, honest, just, pure, lovely, and of good report (Phil. 4:8). Preoccupation with the demonic is potentially harmful. Worse is the attitude that demonology is basically mythology, unworthy of serious consideration. The word "sobriety" forbids such attitudes. "Watchfulness" or "vigilance" specifies an awareness of the wiles of Satan as he makes calculated approaches to believers. The idea seems to urge awareness of his approach.

Furthermore, upon sensing his subtle presence, the disciple is ordered to resist Satan, "steadfast in the faith." "Resist" is a different word from the one used to describe God's resistance to the proud in verse 5. Here the word is *antistēte*, using *anti*, "against," with *histēmi*, meaning "to stand" or "to place." The admonition is to stand firmly against the devil. The method of "standing firm," which Peter advocates, is somewhat different from that espoused by some modern advocates. No word is mentioned about "rebuking" the devil or carrying on conversations with him. The instruction is to resist him "in the faith." By means of sound doctrine and that translated into a militant faith in the God of all providences, Satan may be caused to flee.

The entire discussion of the activities of Satan at this point does not converge around temptations in the form of lust. The milieu of the discussion is still that of Christian suffering. Satan is viewed as the ultimate instigator of persecution and reviling. Peter, therefore, reminds his hearers that they are not alone as the objects of these satanic broadsides. Brethren throughout the world are also seeing these same "sufferings" *(pathēmatōn)* accomplished in them. "Accomplished" is actually a fine translation, although the English sense of "accomplish" only partially catches the import of *epiteleō*. The word really means "to carry through to completion."

Peter's thought is a close approximation to Paul's reference to filling up that which was behind of "the afflictions of Christ" (Col. 1:24). Apparently the suffering of Christians is perceived by the apostles as a necessary concomitant to service to Christ in the world (2 Tim. 3:12). Knowing then that these same things are being carried through to completion everywhere else, Peter's hearers should resist the devil's efforts to intimidate.

Verse 10. "Where sin abounds, there does grace much more abound" (Rom. 5:20). In the midst of suffering and satanic attack, the promise is that the God of all grace is also there. He is the same one who, though allowing us to pass through the deep water, has actually called us "unto his eternal glory" through Jesus Christ. The situation is precisely what Abraham told Dives in Luke 16:19-31. In the lifetime of the rich man he had enjoyed comfort whereas Lazarus knew hardship and rebuff. Now, the situation is completely reversed. The only difference is seventy years versus eternity!

Therefore, Peter promises, after you have suffered a little while, then the God of all grace will do four things. He will (1) make you perfect, (2) stablish, (3) strengthen, and (4) settle you. Note the Greek words with their meanings.

(1) *Katartizō* means "to mend" and is used to describe the mending of nets for fishing.[7] *Artizō* provides our English word "artisan."

---

[7]Criswell, *Expository Sermons*, p. 110.

(2) *Stērizō* means "to strengthen" or "to settle."

(3) *Sthenoō* means "to strengthen."

(4) *Themelioō* means "to lay a foundation" or "to ground firmly." The promise is that the God of all grace will mend and fashion sufferers, rendering them settled, strong, and firmly entrenched.

Verse 11. Mention of what God is going to do prompts a doxology. Peter says, "To him be glory and dominion for ever and ever." The last phrase provides an interesting but inconsequential textual variant. Does Peter's autograph say "for ever" or does it say "for ever and ever"? Based on ancient copies, about as much can be said for one reading as for the other. Whichever is the case, the meaning is exactly the same. The sole difference would be that one reading is a little more emphatic.

The Church of Babylon (5:12-14)

12—By Silvanus, a faithful brother unto you, as I suppose, I have written briefly, exhorting, and testifying that this is the true grace of God wherein ye stand.

13—The church that is at Babylon, elected together with you, saluteth you; and so doth Marcus my son.

14—Greet ye one another with a kiss of charity. Peace be with you all that are in Christ Jesus. Amen.

Verse 12. "By Silvanus" is a simple statement which plunges interpreters into controversy. Three possibilities exist. (1) Peter wrote the epistle and Silvanus is only the postman. (2) Peter virtually dictated the letter with Silvanus serving as amanuensis. (3) The thoughts are definitely those of Peter, but Silvanus was the *hermeneutēs*, the interpreter who exercised great liberty in writing the letter.

The last theory gains plausibility from the fact that Papias mentions this at an early date. Furthermore, the Greek of the epistle is a more erudite style than some imagine within the capability of a fisherman-preacher. On the other hand, Lenski argues persuasively that neither of the last two theories could be correct. He does so, first of all, on the basis of the position of the word *humin*, "to you," in the text. The word certainly does occupy an unusually prominent position in the sentence. Lenski says that the reason is to emphasize Silvanus as bearer of the letter from Peter to his readers.[8] The riddle cannot be solved. The third view, seeing Silvanus as interpreter, would indeed strain the credibility of such statements as Peter's introduction of himself in 1:1. Since we know only that Silvanus was the courier, perhaps it is best to operate with view one as a premise.

Silvanus is almost certainly Silas (his name in Greek), the famous missionary partner of Paul. He appears at the Jerusalem conference in Acts 15:22. He was given the mantle of apostleship by Paul in First Thessalonians 2:6. While he never enjoyed the fame of Peter, James, John, or Paul, he does emerge in sufficient prominence to become better known to us than are most of the original twelve. Peter says that Silvanus is a faithful brother to the recipients of the letter. The apostle has written briefly to them by way of exhortation and testimony concerning the true grace of God in which they stand.

Verse 13. Salutations are provided from two sources. The elect of God in Babylon and Marcus, who is described as Peter's son, both desired to be remembered to the brethren. Selwyn contends that it is unlikely that Peter intends his readers to understand Babylon on the Euphrates River in Mesopotamia. Rome is called "Babylon" in Revelation 17:5,9 and again in 18:2. No doubt exists in those passages that Babylon has become a *soubriquet*, as Selwyn says, for Rome.[9] Evidently, the similarities in moral decadence and world-rule intentions caused Christians to begin to identify the two very early. This intensified when Rome, like Babylon, became a

---

[8]R. C. H. Lenski, *The Interpretation of the Epistles of I and II Peter, the Three Epistles of John, and the Epistle of Jude,* p. 229.
[9]Selwyn, *First Epistle of Saint Peter,* p. 243.

primary agency in the persecution of God's people. The cryptogram "Babylon" as a description of the city of seven hills may have been used first as a method of moral judgment on Rome and later as a means of veiling harsh indictments of the system. While all of this is partially true, the book of First Peter is not an apocalyptic book.

In answer to the arguments of Selwyn and others, the *Criswell Study Bible* note on 5:13 provides an alternative.

Peter is alluding to the Babylon on the Euphrates, a part of that eastern world where he lived and did his work. Those who assert that Babylon is a cryptic word for Rome fail to recognize that: (1) There is no evidence that Rome was ever called Babylon until after the writing of the book of Revelation around 95 A.D., many years after Peter's death. (2) Peter's method and manner of writing are in no sense apocalyptic. On the contrary, Peter is a man plain of speech, almost blunt, who would surely not interject such a mystical allusion into his personal explanations and final salutations. (3) Babylon is no more cryptic than Pontus, Asia, or the rest when Peter says the elect in Babylon send greetings to the Jews of the Dispersion in Pontus, Galatia, Cappadocia, Asia, and Bithynia. (4) Babylon, no longer a great world capital in the time of Peter, was still inhabited by a colony of people, mostly Jews, many of whom Peter befriended and won to Christ. (5) A study of the chronology of Peter's travels further confirms Babylon to be the Babylon on the Euphrates. Such a study reveals these significant points: (a) In 40 A.D., three years after Paul's conversion and subsequent travels into Arabia, Peter was still in Jerusalem. Around that time, he made his missionary journey through the western part of Judea to Lydda, Joppa, Caesarea, and back to Jerusalem (Acts 9—11). (b) Imprisoned under Herod Agrippa I and miraculously delivered by the angel of the Lord (Acts 12), Peter "went down from Judea to Caesarea and there abode" (Acts 12:19). Peter was still in Palestine when Herod Agrippa I died (Acts 12:10-23). The date, according to Josephus, was the fourth year of the reign of Claudius, c. 44 A.D. In 54 A.D., soon after Paul visited Peter again in Jerusalem (Gal. 2), Peter returned the visit by going to Antioch where Paul was working and where the famous interview between the two occurred (Gal. 2:11-14). (c) From 54 A.D. to about 60 A.D., Peter apparently made an extensive missionary journey (or journeys) throughout the Roman provinces of the East, taking his wife with him (1 Cor. 9:5). (d) During their travels in Pontus, Galatia, Cappadocia, Asia, and Bithynia, Peter and his wife remained in the Orient, never entering Rome. One can verify this by the last chapter of the epistle to the church at Rome, written around 58 A.D., in which Paul salutes twenty-seven persons, never mentioning Peter. It is clear that Paul did not send him greetings simply because Peter was neither there, nor ever had been. Those who hold that Peter governed a church at Rome must face the fact of Paul's omission of Peter's name. Had Peter been in Rome, the omission would have been a gross insult. Furthermore, it had been agreed at the Jerusalem Conference that Peter should go to the Jews and Paul to the Gentiles. The church at Rome was Gentile (Rom. 1:13), and Paul was eager to go where no other apostle had been (Rom. 15:20; 2 Cor. 10:15-16). Since he wrote his Roman epistle to the people at Rome, Paul's desire to witness to the Roman city would be inexplicable had Peter been there, or had he been there a number of years. Neither while Paul was under Roman imprisonment from about 60 to 64 A.D., when he wrote four letters to the Gentiles—Ephesians, Philippians, Colossians, and Philemon—nor shortly before his death, when he wrote his final letter to young Timothy, did he mention Peter. In his letters he mentioned many fellow Christians who were in Rome, but clearly he stated in Second Timothy 4:11 that Luke only was with him.[10]

Regarding "Marcus," the sonship which Peter suggests is not biological. Probably, it is not even spiritual, in the sense that Peter introduced John Mark to Christ. The tradition of a close relationship between Peter and John Mark is well known. Many believe that Mark's gospel represents to a large degree the preaching of Simon Peter. Certainly the teacher-pupil relationship had been so close and so widely recognized that it was not unnatural for Peter to speak of Mark as his own son.

"Marcus" almost certainly refers to John Mark whose mother's home in Jerusalem was one of the primary assembly

---

[10]Paige Patterson, "Notes on First Peter," *Criswell Study Bible*, ed. W. A. Criswell (Nashville: Thomas Nelson, 1979), p. 1457.

points for the early church. A home large enough to encompass such meetings hints at some degree of wealth. He is the same young man whose abortive mission effort with Paul and Barnabas became the cause of rift between the two. Later, however, he is apparently in Rome working again with Paul. He figures prominently then in the ministries of Paul, Barnabas, and Peter, and finally as the author of the second gospel.

Verse 14. The concluding remarks of the epistle encourage the greeting of one another with a kiss of love. This is a reference to the same social convention advocated by Paul when he speaks often of "the holy kiss." This kind of greeting was common enough in the ancient Near East even as it is today. However, the warm fellowship which the early Christians enjoyed made the kiss an especially appropriate greeting, thus indicating something of the degree to which they cherished their fellowship.

The epistle concludes with Peter's simple benediction of "peace to all that are in Christ Jesus." Peace *(eirēnē)*, a word which gives us our English word "irenic," does not mean the absence of conflict. Indeed, the whole epistle has dealt with the fact of inevitable Christian suffering from various persecuting hands. "Peace" is the abiding stillness of spirit which God gives in the midst of the storm (Phil. 4:7). However the elements convulse in external turmoil, the pilgrim priesthood is at inner peace in Jesus Christ.

A P P E N D I X

Chart A
Major Historical Perspectives of First Peter 3:18-22

I. Proclamation of a New Opportunity for Either Fallen Angels or Lost Antediluvians or Both
   1. Place - *sheol* or *hades*
   2. Nature of message - gospel of the second chance
   3. Time - between crucifixion and resurrection
   4. Problems
      (a) There are no grounds in either Testament to support the possibility of any opportunity of salvation after death.
      (b) Only universalists or semi-universalists hold this view, doing so because they cannot imagine the coexistence of a gracious God and eternal punishment.
      (c) If the view is correct, why is there no comment as to the success of such an endeavor?
      (d) Scripture teaches precisely the opposite. "It is appointed unto man once to die, and after that the judgment" (Heb. 9:27).

II. Proclamation of Judgment to Antediluvians
   1. Place - *sheol* or *hades*
   2. Nature of message - condemnation
   3. Time - between crucifixion and resurrection
   4. Problems
      (a) No apparent purpose is served by announcing the condemnation of the antediluvians.
      (b) *Kērussō*, "to preach," usually is associated with good news, not bad news.

      (c) If the passage connects with 4:6 and the use of *euangelizomai*, then the idea of "judgment" is certainly absent.

      (d) Why single out the antediluvians rather than including all the lost of the pre-Christian era?

III. Proclamation of Judgment to Fallen Angels
    1. Place - the abyss or *tartarus*
    2. Nature of message - condemnation
    3. Time - between crucifixion and resurrection
    4. Problems
      (a) No apparent purpose is served by announcing angelic condemnation.
      (b) *Kērussō*, "to preach," usually is associated with good news, not bad news.
      (c) While angels are "spirits," so are men (Dan. 7:15; 1 Cor. 5:5; Acts 7:59; Heb. 12:23; Eccl. 12:7); and there is no contextual justification for insisting that these spirits are angels.

IV. Proclamation of the Entire Accomplishment of the Gospel to Old Testament Saints
    1. Place - a division of *sheol* or *hades* known as paradise
    2. Nature of message - the thorough accomplishing (*teleios*) of promised redemption
    3. Time - between crucifixion and resurrection
    4. Problems
      (a) Why are the antediluvians singled out rather than all Old Testament Saints?
      (b) Why did Jesus promise "paradise" to the thief?
      (c) Why did Jesus "commend" His Spirit to God, if in fact *hades* was His destination?
      (d) Why did Paul feel that "absence from the body" was "presence with the Lord?"
      (e) What is the rationale or necessity for this proclamation?
      (f) Where did Enoch and Elijah go when taken bodily from the world?
      (g) Why are they characterized as "disobedient spirits?"

V. Proclamation of the Gospel to Antediluvians by Noah
    1. Place - the antediluvian earth
    2. Nature of message - invitation and exhortation to repentance
    3. Time - the days of Noah

4. Problems
   (a) "He went" (*poreutheis*) seems to imply a personal journey and is a term often associated with death.
   (b) The journey appears to be at the time of Christ's passion.
   (c) If paradise and heaven are synonymous, and if *hades* refers only to a "state" and not to a "place," why utilize these terms in such a confusing way?
   (d) The word "prison" yields better to an understanding of "intermediate state" or even "intermediate place," than to a spiritual condition.
   (e) Is it not true that the appearance of the Old Testament saints at the time of Christ's resurrection is associated with His return from paradise, the godly realm of *hades*?

Chart B
Exegetical Possibilities for First Peter 3:18-22 and 4:6

First Peter 3:18-22
v. 18 "Quickened by the Spirit"
   (1) Made alive "in" the Spirit - a reference to resurrection.
   (2) Made alive "by" the Spirit - a reference to a condition of His Spirit immediately after His bodily death.
v. 19 (1) "He went"
      (a) A journey to the underworld made after the crucifixion
      (b) A spiritual journey in the days of Noah in which Christ preached through Noah
   (2) "and preached"
      (a) *kērussō* = to proclaim a second chance
      (b) *kērussō* = to proclaim judgment
      (c) *kērussō* = to proclaim victory
      (d) *kērussō* = to proclaim release
      (e) *kērussō* = to proclaim salvation contingent upon repentance and faith
   (3) "to the Spirits"
      (a) Fallen angels
      (b) Disembodied Old Testament saints
      (c) Rebellious of Noah's period now confined to *hades* awaiting judgment
      (d) Men in the flesh whose "spirits" are confronted in the preaching of Noah
   (4) "in prison"
      (a) Angels reserved in chains of darkness in the abyss or *tartarus*

        (b) Old Testament saints in *hades* (paradise)

        (c) Men imprisoned by their sins

        (d) Old Testament sinners confined in *hades*

v. 20 (1) "were disobedient"

        (a) Fallen angels from Satan's rebellion

        (b) Fallen angels from an antediluvian rebellion

        (c) Antediluvian men

   (2) "In the days of Noah"

        (a) Reference to fallen angels

        (b) Reference to antediluvians of Noah's time

        (c) Antediluvians mentioned as symbolic of those to whom Christ preached

First Peter 4:6

   (1) "The gospel was preached" *(euēngelishthē)*

        (a) Is the statement related to 3:18f? If so, there is either a second chance offered or else the passage has reference to men in Noah's day.

        (b) Is the statement related to the present preaching of gospel?

        (c) Is the passage unrelated to First Peter 3:19f?

   (2) "to those who are dead"

        (a) Reference to the spirits in prison who are dead physically

        (b) Reference to those dead in trespasses and sin

Chart C
A Theological Persuasion Concerning First Peter 3:18-22

1. The program of God, in a sense, has been the same throughout history, i.e., to bring about the redemption of lost men at His own personal cost (grace) on the basis of repentance toward God and faith in God's salvific provision.

2. This may be seen most clearly in the sufferings of Jesus on the cross (v. 18), but also in the efforts exerted by the Spirit of Christ in the days of Noah (vv. 19-20). (Peter demonstrates uncommon interest in the flood and the antediluvian civilization.)

3. The same Spirit which made Christ alive through the resurrection (v. 18) preached to those imprisoned by their sins, i.e., Noah's contemporaries, (vv. 19-20) through Noah himself. Noah was a "preacher of righteousness" (2 Peter 2:5). Whatever preaching was done had to be the gospel because that is the general use of *kērussō* and always of *euangelizomai* in 4:6.

4. In spite of God's longsuffering, there were only seven converts

who were saved out of the decadent society in the midst of the rising waters of the flood.

5. Baptism is a figure *(antitupos)* of the deliverance of a soul from the power and presence of sin in a manner similar to the deliverance of Noah and his family from the flood.

Spiritual and Pragmatic Values of the Passage
Regardless of Exegetical Minutiae

1. Our Lord does not forget His creation but tenderly, selflessly, compassionately seeks man's good.

2. Death is of only relative consequence to Christ and His people.

3. Baptism is the public antitype of salvation, providing a beautiful picture of deliverance from sin.

4. Christ reigns as Sovereign over seen and unseen worlds regardless of apparent chaos.

BIBLIOGRAPHY

Selected References on First Peter

Alford, Henry. *The Greek Testament with a Critically Revised Text, A Digest of Various Readings, Marginal References to Verbal and Idiomatic Usage, Prolegomena, and a Critical and Exegetical Commentary.* Volume IV. Chicago: Moody Press, 1958.

Barclay, William. *The Letters of James and Peter.* Philadelphia: Westminster Press, 1960.

Baxter, J. Sidlow. *Explore the Book.* Volume VI. Grand Rapids: Zondervan, 1962.

————. *Studies in Problem Texts.* Grand Rapids: Zondervan, 1968.

Bigg, Charles. *A Critical and Exegetical Commentary on the Epistles of St. Peter and St. Jude* in the *International Critical Commentary.* Edinburgh: T. & T. Clark, 1961.

Blair, J. Allen. *Living Peacefully: A Devotional Study of the First Epistle of Peter.* Neptune, New Jersey: Loizeaux Bros., 1959.

Brown, John. *Expository Discourses on I Peter.* Volume II. Edinburgh: The Banner of Truth Trust, 1975.

Calvin, John. *Commentaries on The Epistle of Paul the Apostle to the Hebrews.* Volume XXII. Grand Rapids: Baker Book House, 1979.

Carroll, B. H. *An Interpretation of the English Bible: The Pastoral Epistles of Paul, 1 and 2 Peter, Jude, and 1, 2, and 3 John.* Volume XVI. Nashville: Broadman Press, 1947.

Clark, Gordon H. *Peter Speaks Today: A Devotional Commentary on First Peter.* Philadelphia: Presbyterian and Reformed Publishing Co., 1967.

Criswell, W. A. *Expository Sermons on the Epistles of Peter.* Grand Rapids: Zondervan, 1976.

Darby, J. N. *Synopsis of the Books of the Bible.* Volume 5. Winschoten, Netherlands: H. L. Heijkoop, 1970.

Ellicott, Charles John. *Ellicott's Commentary on the Whole Bible.* Volume VIII. Grand Rapids: Zondervan, 1981.

Elliott, John H. *A Home for the Homeless: A Sociological Exegesis of I Peter, Its Situation and Strategy.* Philadelphia: Fortress Press, 1981.

Exell, Joseph S. *The Biblical Illustrator: I Peter.* Grand Rapids: Baker Book House, 1958.

————, and H. D. M. Spence, eds. *The Pulpit Commentary.* Volume 22. Grand Rapids: Wm. B. Eerdmans Publishing Co., 1958.

Gaebelein, Frank E. *The Expositor's Bible Commentary.* Volume 12. Grand Rapids: Zondervan, 1981.

Hart, J. H. A. *The First Epistle General of Peter* in *The Expositor's Greek Testament.* Volume V. Grand Rapids: Wm. B. Eerdmans Publishing Co., 1951.

Ironside, H. A. *Expository Notes on the Epistles of James and Peter.* New York: Loizeaux Bros., 1947.

Jowett, J. H. *The Epistles of St. Peter: A Practical and Devotional Commentary.* Grand Rapids: Kregel Publications, 1970.

Lange, J. P. *Commentary on the Holy Scriptures.* Grand Rapids: Zondervan, 1960.

Leighton, Robert. *Commentary on First Peter.* Grand Rapids: Kregel Publications, 1972.

Lenski, R. C. H. *The Interpretation of the Epistles of I and II Peter, the Three Epistles of John, and the Epistle of Jude.* Minneapolis: Augsburg Publishing House, 1966.

Meyer, F. B. *Tried by Fire: Expositions of the First Epistle of Peter.* Edinburgh: Marshall, Morgan & Scott, 1955.

Nieboer, J. *Practical Exposition of 1 Peter Verse by Verse.* North East, Pennsylvania: Our Daily Walk, 1951.

Pelikan, Jaraslav, ed. *Luther's Works,* Volume 30. St. Louis: Concordia Publishing House, 1967.

Reicke, Bo. *The Disobedient Spirits and Christian Baptism: A Study of 1 Peter III. 19 and Its Context.* Printed in Sweden, 1946.

————. *The Epistles of James, Peter, and Jude* in *The Anchor Bible.* Volume 37. Garden City, New York: Doubleday & Co., 1964.

Selwyn, Edward Gordon. *The First Epistle of St. Peter.* London: Macmillan & Co., 1964.

Stibbs, Alan M. *The First Epistle General of Peter.* Grand Rapids: Wm. B. Eerdmans Publishing Co., 1959.

Summers, Ray. *The Broadman Bible Commentary.* Volume 12. Nashville: Broadman Press, 1972.

Wuest, Kenneth S. *First Peter in the Greek New Testament.* Grand Rapids: Wm. B. Eerdmans Publishing Co., 1942.

Other Works Cited

Barth, Karl. *Church Dogmatics.* Volume IV, Part 2. Edinburgh: T. & T. Clark, 1967.

Brown, Francis, S. R. Driver, and C. A. Briggs. *Hebrew and English Lexicon of the Old Testament.* Oxford: Clarendon Press, 1962.

Buswell, James Oliver. *A Systematic Theology of the Christian Religion.* Grand Rapids: Zondervan, 1962.

Dana, H. E., and Julius R. Mantey. *A Manual Grammar of the Greek New Testament.* New York: Macmillan & Co., 1960.

Fisher, Milton C. *Theological Wordbook of the Old Testament.* Volume 2. Edited by R. Laird Harris, Gleason L. Archer, and Bruce K. Waltke. Chicago: Moody Press, 1980.

Fletcher, Joseph. *Situation Ethics: The New Morality.* Philadelphia: Westminster Press, 1966.

Humphreys, Fisher. *The Death of Christ.* Nashville: Broadman Press, 1978.

Kittel, Gerhard, ed. *Theological Dictionary of the New Testament.* Grand Rapids: Wm. B. Eerdmans Publishing Co., 1967.

Liddell, Henry George, and Robert Scott. *A Greek-English Lexicon.* Oxford: Clarendon Press, 1966.

Lightfoot, J. B. *The Epistle of St. Paul to the Galatians* in the *Classic Commentary Library.* Grand Rapids: Zondervan, 1962.

MacCulloch, J. A. *The Harrowing of Hell: A Comparative Study of an Early Christian Doctrine.* Edinburgh: T. & T. Clark, 1930.

Mikolaski, Samuel J. *The Grace of God.* Grand Rapids: Wm. B. Eerdmans Publishing Co., 1966.

Moody, Dale. *The Word of Truth.* Grand Rapids: Wm. B. Eerdmans Publishing Co., 1981.

Morris, Leon. *The Apostolic Preaching of the Cross.* Grand Rapids: Wm. B. Eerdmans Publishing Co., 1965.

———. *The Cross in the New Testament.* Grand Rapids: Wm. B. Eerdmans Publishing Co., 1965.

Moulton, James Hope, and George Milligan. *The Vocabulary of the Greek Testament.* Grand Rapids: Wm. B. Eerdmans Publishing Co., 1974.

Nygren, Anders. *Agape and Eros.* Philadelphia: Westminster Press, 1953.

Patterson, Paige. *The Shophar Papers.* Volume 2, "Authority and the Priesthood of the Believer." Dallas: Criswell Center for Biblical Studies (525 N. Ervay, Dallas, TX 75201), 1980.

Pollock, J. C. *The Faith of the Russian Evangelicals.* New York: McGraw-Hill Book Co., 1964.

Roberts, Alexander, and James Donaldson. *The Ante-Nicene Fathers.* Volume I. Grand Rapids: Wm. B. Eerdmans Publishing Co., 1973.

Robertson, A. T. *A Grammar of the Greek New Testament in the Light of Historical Research.* Nashville: Broadman Press, 1934.

Robinson, John A. T. *Honest to God.* Philadelphia: Westminster Press, 1963.

Schaeffer, Francis A. *A Christian Manifesto.* Westchester, Illinois: Crossway Books, 1982.

Schaff, Philip, and Henry Wace. *A Select Library of Nicene and Post-Nicene Fathers of the Christian Church.* Second Series. Volume I. Grand Rapids: Wm. B. Eerdmans Publishing Co., 1971.

Spurgeon, C. H. *The Metropolitan Tabernacle Pulpit.* Pasadena, Texas: Pilgrim Publications, 1978.

Strong, Augustus Hopkins. *Systematic Theology.* Philadelphia: Judson Press, 1960.

Thayer, Joseph Henry. *A Greek-English Lexicon of the New Testament.* New York: American Book Company, 1889.

Trench, Richard C. *Synonyms of the New Testament.* Grand Rapids: Wm. B. Eerdmans Publishing Co., 1975.

Verduin, Leonard. *The Reformers and Their Stepchildren.* Grand Rapids: Wm. B. Eerdmans Publishing Co., 1964.